THE MYSTICAL DIMENSION

Volume I:

THE MYSTICAL TRADITION

THE MYSTICAL DIMENSION
Volume One

The Mystical Tradition

Insights into the Nature of
The Mystical Tradition in Judaism

by

Jacob Immanuel Schochet

Second Edition

KEHOT PUBLICATION SOCIETY
770 Eastern Parkway, New York 11213
5755 • 1995

Kehot Publication Society
770 Eastern Parkway / Brooklyn, New York 11213
(718) 774-4000 / FAX (718) 774-2718

Orders:
291 Kingston Avenue / Brooklyn, New York 11213
(718) 778-0226 / FAX (718) 778-4148

Library of Congress Cataloging-in-Publication Data
Schochet, Jacob Immanuel
  The Mystical dimension / by Jacob Immanuel Schochet
  550 p. 15x221/2 cm.
    Includes bibliographical references and index.
    Contents: v. 1. The mystical tradition -- v. 2. Deep calling
unto deep -- v. 3. Chassidic dimensions
      ISBN 0-8266-0528-1 (v. 1)
      ISBN 0-8266-0529-X (v. 2)
      ISBN 0-8266-0530-3 (v. 3)
      1. Mysticism--Judaism. 2. Prayer--Judaism. 3. Repentance--
Judaism. 4. Hasidism. 5. Judaism. I. Title.
BM723.S338   1990   90-4090
296.7'12--cd20   CIP

Printed in the United States of America

בס"ד

לזכות

רחל בת יעלא אסתר

שתליט"א

אשת חיל עטרת בעלה

The Mystical Tradition

Table of Contents

PREFACE

Over the course of the past few decades I was invited to deliver numerous lectures about the history and teachings of Jewish mysticism, and particularly of Chassidism. At the same time I also published a number of books, essays and studies in those fields. By virtue of the great and increasing interest in Jewish mysticism, many people have urged me for years to gather and publish these lectures and essays in one depository for ready access.

For most of the lectures, however, I have at best very brief notes of key-words and some references, except for those that were recorded by listeners. Also, most of the articles and essays, written over the course of close to three decades, are in need of updating or revisions. The great amount of time and effort required for producing transcripts, and for editing and revising all materials, prevented me from undertaking this task. On the other hand, there are troubling strictures relating to "He who withholds 'corn'..."

(Proverbs 11:26), as interpreted by our sages.[1] Thus I started gradually with a selection of materials for which there has been a greater demand, to produce this initial series of three volumes on the mystical dimension in Judaism.

The essays and studies in these volumes deal essentially with explanations of the mystical tradition and perspective in general. The emphasis is on themes and topics that are both central and practical in Chassidic thought. Most of the material was revised, and updated with references to presently readily accessible editions of sources. Occasional overlapping of some themes and ideas is to be expected. More often than not, however, these "repetitions" complement or supplement one another. In view of the fact that this is a collection of essays and studies composed at separate and varying times, there is disparity and inconsistency in the transliteration of non-English words and the rendition of names (e.g., in some parts *Rambam*, and in others *Maimonides; Joseph* and *Yosef*; and so forth).

The copious footnotes should not scare off the average reader by giving the appearance of a technical text. These volumes do not represent original insights of the author. They are no more than an attempt to present ideas and teachings of old. Most of the notes thus simply present my sources. Other notes explain or qualify the text, or offer further elaborations.

The numerous quotations from, or references to, Talmud, Midrashim, Zohar, and early classical sources, are not intended as a display of erudition. They simply demonstrate

---

1. *Sanhedrin* 91b. See *Zohar* III:46b; *Sefer Chassidim*, section 530, and the commentaries *ad loc. Cf. Rosh Hashanah* 23a; *Sukah* 49b; *Vayikra Rabba* 22:1; *et passim*.

how the cited teachings of Chassidism, especially its alleged innovations, are firmly rooted in the historical tradition of normative Judaism.

The modern trend is to put footnotes at the end of chapters, or of the whole book, to avoid the appearance of an overly technical text. Personally I find this awkward. Taking advantage of an author's prerogative, I applied my preference for footnotes in the margins of the relevant passages to more readily serve their purposes.

In view of the intended aims of these volumes, the citations of Chassidic thoughts and teachings generally concentrate on the original sources of the early masters, more particularly — the teachings of R. Israel Baal Shem Tov and his successor, R. Dov Ber, the Maggid of Mezhirech. Bibliographical details for texts cited appear in the index.

The mystical tradition is the most delicate part of our Torah. Thus it is the author's fervent prayer to be spared of errors in this undertaking. By the same token he hopes also that these volumes will contribute somewhat to the goal of illuminating the world with the light of *pnimiyut Hatorah*. This will of itself speed the Messianic promise of "The earth shall be filled with the knowledge of G-d as the waters cover the sea" (Isaiah 11:9), "and they shall teach no more every man his neighbour and every man his brother saying, 'Know G-d,' for they shall *all* know Me, from the least of them unto the greatest of them" (Jeremiah 31:33).[2]

J. I. S.

---

2. *Zohar* III:23a; Rambam, *Hilchot Teshuvah* 9:2, and *Hilchot Melachim* 12:5.

Bibliographical notes for The Mystical Dimension

Volume One: The Mystical Tradition

"To Be One With The One": Combination of revised article published in 1971 and transcripts of lectures.

"Jewish Mysticism: Authentic Tradition vs. Subjective Intuitions": Edited transcript of lecture delivered at the International Symposium of Jewish Mysticism, Oxford (England) May 1981.

"Let Your Well-Springs Be Dispersed Abroad": The text of the first seven chapters appeared first in *Di Yiddishe Heim* XVIII:4 (Spring 5737), then with notes as Foreword to the 3rd edition of *Mystical Concepts in Chassidism* (1979). The present edition is a slightly emended version of the original, with the addition of the last three chapters.

Volume Two: "Deep Calling Unto Deep"

"The Dynamics of Prayer": Revised and expanded version of a series of articles that appeared in *Di Yiddishe Heim* V:2-VI:4 (Fall 5724 — Summer 5725).

"The Dynamics of *Teshuvah*": Edited transcript of a lecture delivered at the International Symposium of Jewish Mysticism — Oxford (England) May 1981 — with the addition of notes.

Volume Three: Chassidic Dimensions

"The Dynamics of *Ahavat Yisrael*": Revised combination of part of an article that appeared in *Tradition* XVI:4 (Summer 1977) and a series of articles that appeared in

Di Yiddishe Heim VIII:3-IX:2 (Winter 5727 — Fall 5728).

"The Concept of the *Rebbe-Tzadik* in Chassidism": Edited transcripts of lectures with the addition of notes.

"Serve G-d With Joy..": Revised and expanded edition of an article that appeared in *Di Yiddishe Heim* XXV:3 (Spring 5746), with the addition of notes.

"Religious Duty And Religious Experience In Chassidism": Revised edition, with the addition of notes, of an article that appeared in *Di Yiddishe Heim* XIV:3 (Winter 5733) to mark the bicentennial of the passing of the Maggid of Mezhirech.

"Lamplighters: The Philosophy of Lubavitch Activism": Slightly revised articles that appeared in *Di Yiddishe Heim* XIV:1-2 (Summer — Fall 5733), and *Tradition* XIII:1 (Summer 1972).

FOREWORD

The existence of a mystical dimension and tradition in Judaism is a well-established fact. In the popular mind, however, this gives rise to all kinds of perceptions. The very mention of "mysticism," or "Kabbalah," oftentimes evokes images of magic, amulets, incantations, spirits, or other non-natural phenomena. These images, in turn, generate different reactions. On one extreme are those so fascinated that they would like to delve into the secret world of the mystics to enable them to manipulate the natural order of things. On the other extreme there are those who, under the guise of would-be rationalism, dismiss the very concept as no more than primitive fantasies and superstitions rooted in ignorance or naivete.

To be sure, there is such a thing as *Kabbalah ma'asit*, "practical Kabbalah," with a system and techniques transcending the natural order. Its authenticity, however, is tested by its dependence on *Kabbalah iyunit*, the philosophical theory and perspective of Jewish mysticism, which in turn is restricted to the boundaries of the totality of Jewish tradition.

Kabbalah *per se* centers on the principle of the omnipresent reality of G-d. The authentic mystic seeks to "touch" the Divine and to become absorbed therein. He does not look for power. Pursuit of self-enhancement or the ability to manipulate is alien to him. His goal is self-effacement, a transcendence of the transient values of material and temporal reality. *Kabbalah ma'asit* on its own is the very opposite thereof, and in the view of the true mystic must therefore be shunned as dangerous and counter-productive.[1]

Kabbalah iyunit presents a complete — albeit complex — system of ontology, cosmogony and cosmology. Many of its central doctrines, such as *tzimtzum, Sefirot, Olamot, Orot, Keilim, Partzufim,* and so forth, are dealt with in my *Mystical Concepts In Chassidism.* In this volume we shall deal with the general nature and perspective of Jewish Mysticism, its place within normative Judaism, the unique aspects that distinguish it from its non-Jewish counterpart, and the significance of its propagation and popularization. The other volumes in this series will deal with more specific aspects of its teachings which affect the practical level of life.

J. Immanuel Schochet

Toronto, Ont., 10th of Shevat, 5750

---

1. See the strict warnings of R. Isaac Luria (the *Ari*) in R. Chaim Vital, *Sha'ar Hamitzvot,* Shemot; *idem., Likutei Torah,* Shemot (*Ta'amei Hamitzvot*); and *Sha'ar Ru'ach Hakodesh,* p. 41, *s.v.* Tikun III. See also *Sefer Chassidim,* par. 204-205, and the sources cited there in *Chassdei Olam and Mekor Chessed;* R. Mosheh Cordovero, *Pardes Rimonim,* Sha'ar XXVII:end of ch. 27; and *cf.* R. Chaim Yosef David Azulay (Chida), *Petach Einayim* on *Avot* 1:13.

"To Be One With The One"

On The Meaning And Relevance Of Jewish Mysticism

"To Be One With The One":

On the Meaning and Relevance
Jewish Mysticism

Table of Contents

"To Be One With The One"

On The Meaning And Relevance Of Jewish Mysticism

"To be one with the One, and thus is established the mystery of 'On that day G-d shall be One and His Name One' (Zechariah 14:9)"

Zohar II:135a

Introduction

Mystics and their followers are often asked what the Kabbalah and Chassidism can tell us today. Considering that Jewish mysticism gained prominence relatively late, of what concern, then, is it to the 'historical Jew'? To be sure, the Jewish mystical tradition goes back to Biblical times and is firmly rooted in the Talmud and Midrashim. Nonetheless, we must recognize the fact that it was generally kept concealed, with involvement restricted to a select group of sages. Why then the 'flood' of mystical writings and teachings in modern times, the attempts to popularize the mystic tradition?

Such questions have been asked (and were anticipated)

21

ever since the mystics removed the screens that restricted their teachings to *yechidei segulah*, a chosen few initiates. Once they furthered their aim by publishing introductory tracts and expositions, they spent a good number of pages to deal with the answers.[1] They trace the historical roots and validity of the Kabbalah and its integral place within normative Judaism. They demonstrate the new vistas it opens, which prove to be of great philosophical, moral as well as Halachic consequence. They stress the fact that these teachings *could* and *should* be publicized and popularized, especially in the sixth millennium which is *ikveta deMeshicha*, the era on the very heels of the Messianic redemption.[2]

Their answers, though well-seasoned by age, are no less relevant to our day and age than to theirs. But before indicating a few symptomatic aspects from this vast realm of thought, some points of clarification are in order. Hopefully they will help hurdle some oft-held misconceptions that stand in the way of appreciating our mystical tradition.

Kabbalah: Jewish Tradition

First of all, our sole concern is with *Jewish* mysticism,

---

1. See, e.g., the works of R. Meir Ibn Gabbai; R. Mosheh Cordovero; R. Chaim Vital; R. Joseph Ergas; and so forth. See also R. Isaac ben Immanuel de Lattes's approbation for the first printing of the *Zohar*; R. Abraham Azulay's Introduction to *Or Hachamah*; and R. Shneur Zalman of Liadi, *Tanya*, Igeret Hakodesh, sect. XXVI. *Cf.* "On the Study and Propagation of *Pnimiyut Hatorah*."
2. On this term and its significance, see *Sotah* 49b; R. Chaim ibn Atar, *Or Hachayim* on Genesis 49:9 and on Deuteronomy 7:12. For an interesting source for this timing, in addition to the references in note 1, see Rambam, *Igeret Teyman*, ed. Kapach, p. 49.

and this includes the authoritative Kabbalah and Chassidism as one. That some of its ideas may be found elsewhere as well, in non-Jewish sources (such as Platonism and Eastern Mysticism), is interesting but *irrelevant*. Alleged common sources, textual criticism, arguments about temporal priority and 'who was influenced by who,' may be fascinating hunting-grounds for the 'mysticist,' offering unlimited scope for speculative theories and hypotheses, but they are of no practical significance whatsoever.

Jewish mysticism, as Judaism in general, does not claim exclusive rights to all insights: "Should a person tell you that there is wisdom among the nations, believe it!"[3] No less a source than the *Zohar*, the basic text of Jewish mysticism, interprets the Midrashic comment that the words "without blemish" (Numbers 19:2) can be applied to the Greeks, "because they are very close to the way of the (true) Faith, more than any of the others."[4] Commentators on the *Zohar* note that this refers specifically to the pre-Aristotelians whose views coincide in some respects with those of our tradition.[5]

The *Zohar* already recognizes that a number of ideas and concepts of Eastern philosophies "are close to the teachings of the Torah." Yet the *Zohar* cautions to stay away from their works in order not to be drawn to their idolatrous ideas and practices, lest one be led away from the service of G-d: "All those books mislead people. For the people of the East used to be sages who had inherited their wisdom from Abraham. He had given it to the children of his concubines, as it is written, 'To the children of his concubines Abraham

---

3. *Eichah Rabba* 2:13.
4. *Zohar* II:237a. *Zohar Chadash*, Yitro: 38b.
5. See R. Joseph Ergas, *Shomer Emunim* I:37.

gave gifts, and he sent them .. to the land of the East'
(Genesis 25:6). Later on, however, they were drawn to many
(idolatrous) sides with their wisdom.''[6]

The point is that Jewish mysticism is *Kabbalah*, in the
literal sense of that word: a source- and time-hallowed
tradition, strictly within the framework of historical, normative Judaism. Its masters are the recognized authoritative
teachers of both Talmudic and later times, and all its premises and doctrines are within, and subject to, Torah and
Halachah. It is part of *Torah shebe'al peh*, the Oral Tradition, and like the other parts thereof has authoritative objec-
tivity and legitimacy as an authentic and integral part of
Judaism proper.[7]

The intimate relationship with, and dependency on,
Halachah, cannot be emphasized sufficiently. A favourite
contention of the 'mysticist,' as erroneous as it is ignorant
and mischievous, creates an imaginary tension between
Halachah and Kabbalah. There is no ground whatsoever for
this contention. Authentic Jewish mysticism is inseparable
from Halachah. It could hardly be different when noting

---

6. *Zohar* I:100a-b. See *Sanhedrin* 91b; and *Torah Shelemah* on
   Genesis 25:6. Note also *Zohar Chadash*, Bereishit: 10d (and *cf.*
   Avodah Zara 55a) why G-d allows some efficacy to idolatrous
   practices and shrines which are altogether prohibited by the
   Torah (a principle comparable to the premise of G-d allowing
   miracles to be performed by false prophets, as stated in
   Deuteronomy 13:2*ff.*).
7. The objective character of mysticism is perceived in the strict
   insistence on total dependence on an authentic chain of tradition
   for all its premises; see Ramban, Introduction to his commentary on the Torah, and his commentary on Genesis 1:1; R.
   Joseph Albo, *Ikkarim* 2:29; R. Meir ibn Gabbai, *Tola'at Ya'a-
   kov*, Introduction; R. Chaim Vital, Introduction to *Eitz
   Chayim*.

how much of the Kabbalistic and Chassidic writings relate Halachic concepts and details to the mystical view of cosmic reality and the interactions between the spiritual and the mundane. Suffice it to note that most of the greatest Halachic authorities and codifiers were also Kabbalists.[8]

This fundamental principle was emphasized by the authorities of all ages, and most acutely so by two of the greatest giants in both Halachah and Kabbalah in recent times: R. Chaim of Voloszin quotes his master R. Elijah of Vilna, known as the *Gaon*, to the effect that it is absolutely impossible to speak of a contradiction between the Talmud and *Zohar*, between the exoteric (revealed) and the esoteric (mystical) facets of the Torah.[9] R. Hillel of Paritsh quotes R. Shneur Zalman of Liadi, known as the *Rav*, to the effect that it is inconceivable that the mystics contradict the Talmud or the *posskim* (codifiers) who derive their decisions from the Talmud.[10]

---

8. E.g., R. Abraham ibn Daud (Rabad of Posquieres); R. Mosheh ben Nachman (Ramban); R. Shelomoh ibn Aderet (Rashba); R. Joseph Karo (Bet Yossef); R. Mosheh Isserles (Rema); R. Mordechai Yaffeh (Levush); and numerous others.

9. See the quotations and references cited in B. Landau, *Hagaon Hachassid MeVilna*, Jerusalem 1967, pp. 140-1.

10. R. Abraham Lavut, *Sha'ar Hakolel*, ch. 1 (quoted in recent editions of *Shulchan Aruch Harav*, vol. I, p. 368), see there.

   This is not to deny that there are some differences between Talmud-Halachah and *Zohar*-Kabbalah. In this context the codifiers rule that in case of a 'conflict' between the exoteric and esoteric traditions we are to follow the former (see *Magen Avraham* on *Orach Chayim* 25:11; Rav's *Shulchan Aruch*, ibid., par. 28; R. Chaim Kobrin, *Tav Chayim*, Kelalim:14. Though see some qualifications in *Sha'ar Hakolel*, ad loc., which parallel the arguments in R. Judah Barzilai, *Perush Sefer Yetzirah*, p. 157; and Responsa *Chacham Tzvi*, no. 36).

Even as *Halachah* stripped of the mystical dimension is
like a body without a soul, so is the mystical tradition
separated from *Halachah*, at best, like a soul without a body
— aimlessly floating about in a void.[11]

Mysticism: Another Dimension

Secondly: An objective view and appreciation of mysticism needs first and foremost an opening of the mind, a
sincere and complete commitment to the pursuit of truth, no
less than one must be prepared to give to the study of any
other branch of knowledge. An appreciation of mysticism
may require a reorientation of thought and attitude from
what we are attuned to by a background and approach that
focuses completely on practicality and empirical understanding. With the Kabbalah and Chassidism one does not
enter a new or different world but a new and different
dimension of one and the same world, a different plane of

Generally speaking, this follows upon the same principle
underlying Halachic disagreements in the exoteric Torah itself.
Of this it is said that both opinions are 'the words of the living
G-d.' They are different dimensions of one and the same tradition, thus both objectively valid (see *Eruvin* 13b, and the commentaries there, especially *Ritba*; Rashi on *Ketuvot* 57a;
commentaries on *Avot* 5:16; and R. Isaiah Horowitz, *Shenei
Luchot Haberit*, Bet Chochmah (end of p. 19a)). For pragmatic
reasons, however, we must rule one way or another, and Halachah is governed by specific rules for its workings and decision-
making process. Thus, for example, while presently we rule
according to Bet Hillel against Bet Shammai, in the Messianic
age we shall adopt the view of Bet Shammai against that of Bet
Hillel; see *Mikdash Melech* on *Zohar* I:17b; R. Shneur Zalman
of Liadi, *Likutei Torah*, Korach, p. 54b-c.

11. R. Chaim Vital, *Eitz Chayim*, Introduction; see below, section
VI, and especially notes 29 and 31.

thought that transcends previously held modes and categories.

One must cast away the prejudices imposed by rationalism and scientism. At the very least one must allow a measure of admissibility to the possibility of an order of reality that is not our normative phenomenal one, and allow the possibility of methods of perception that differ from our usual ones. This will indeed reduce our phenomenal world to no more than a partial reality; but surely it would be highly unscientific to deny these possibilities. The sincere pursuit of true knowledge is subject to a sense of humility. There must be a willingness to surrender the ego of self-assurance and to override personal bias. In the words of our sages: " 'Pay close attention to all the words .. because *it is no vain thing for you*' (Deuteronomy 32:46-47) — if it *does* appear to be a 'vain thing,' it is so 'for you,' *because of you*," because of the deficiency in your apprehension![12]

A classical precedent for this principle is found in the following passage from the *Gemara*: When R. Zeyra left to ascend to the Holy Land, he fasted one hundred fasts in order to forget the methodology of the Babylonian Talmud so that it would not trouble him in the study and acquisition of the Jerusalem Talmud.[13]

To put all this into perspective, it will do well to

---

12. *Sifre*, Ekev, end of par. 48; *Yerushalmi*, *Pe'ah* 1:1; *Bereishit Rabba* 1:14 (cited in Rambam, *Moreh Nevuchim* III: ch. 26 and 50). In this context it would do well to ponder also the acute premise underlying Rambam's defense of *creatio ex nihilo* (*Moreh Nevuchim* II:17) and his treatment of the problem of evil (*ibid.* III:12).

13. *Baba Metzia* 85a (see commentaries there, and R. Judah Loew (Maharal), *Netivot Olam*, Netiv Hatorah, ch. 13). This source

ponder a parable of the Baal Shem Tov: A musician once played a beautiful melody with immensely moving sweetness. The beauty of that music so enraptured the listeners that they were unable to control themselves and felt compelled to leap and dance, almost reaching the ceiling. The closer one came to the musician, there was a pull to move still closer the better to hear, attaining ever greater pleasure and dancing ever more.

In the midst of all this, a deaf man entered. Unable to hear the beautiful music, he could not appreciate what was happening. All he perceived was people dancing intensely and a man on stage motioning strangely with some kind of instrument in his hands. To his mind they were all mad. He thought to himself: "What kind of celebration is going on here?"

Now if this deaf man were wise, he would realize and understand that those people were moved by the beauty and pleasantness of the musical sounds coming from the instrument, and he, too, would have danced. The moral is obvious...[14]

Mysticism vs. Scientism

Thirdly: The modern attitude to the universe is one of

---

is doubly apt, because the basic distinctions between the Jerusalem Talmud and the Babylonian Talmud (see *Sanhedrin* 24a; *Zohar Chadash*, Eichah: 93a; Rashi, *Chagigah* 10a, *s.v.* afilu; *Chidushei Haritva*, *Yoma* 57a; and my notes on *Likkutei Sichot* (English), vol. III: Vayikra, p. 70*f.*) are acutely descriptive of the two perspectives we are dealing with here.

14. Quoted in R. Mosheh Chaim Ephrayim of Sudylkov (grandson and disciple of the Baal Shem Tov), *Degel Machaneh Ephrayim*, Yitro (*Sefer Baal Shem Tov*, Yitro, par. 55).

rational inquiry. It seeks in the phenomenal world — its sole realm of concern — a scientific uniformity to which all facts and factors must conform. The search is endless, but this does not deter the scientist. He refuses to admit defeat or the possibility of exception to his underlying scientific premises. 'Scientism' and would-be 'objective rationalism' thus often slide into an uncritical dogmatism second to none, and a new 'religion' is born: a 'religion' of ever-new and changing revelations, with an endless chain of 'high-priests' reflecting the moods, conditions and revelations of their times.

There is a degree of legitimacy in this approach. Despite its glaring shortcomings, it is to be credited for tremendous technological advances. Nonetheless, in attempting to establish his type of uniformity, the modern rationalist paradoxically creates, in effect, an increasingly disturbing pluralism and an alienating divisiveness. Even as he converts the universe into a mammoth machine, he breaks it up into innumerable particles, separate from — and non-related to — one another. His physiomonistic pantheism concerns itself only with species and universals. Individual identities become sacrifices for the sustenance of his *deus in machina*. The human individual (as well as any other particulars) diminishes in proportion to the growth of nature and the universe in the scientific, experimental grasp or consciousness. Human individual life is hedged in by a precarious day-to-day, here-and-now, existence.

Some may take this as a stark fact of life. There is, however, an intuitive categorical and transcending sense of morality deeply embedded in the soul and mind of man (and often emboldened by a host of empirical facts) which revolts against this callous materialism which leaves us with nothing but barren factualism. The resulting tension between the haunting Lorelei of modern rational inquiry and the groping attempts at human self-assertion lies at the root of many, if not all, of our present-day neuroses and vexations, and "he that increases knowledge increases pain."

The apparent alternatives are resignation or rejection: resignation to the admittedly frustrating paradox, and making the best of it, or the elimination of either the modern method or the recognition of individuality. Obviously, neither of these choices is satisfactory. At this point mysticism offers a viable solution, a new approach. No doubt that this accounts for the recent popularity of mysticism, in both legitimate and illegitimate forms. From our point of view, however, this viable alternative is at best an incidental fringe-benefit.

Jewish mysticism did not come into being to be a panacea for social, mental or emotional problems.[15] As already stated, it is an integral part of Torah, an authentic part of Divine Revelation and instruction. It is part of the tradition that is subject to the *mitzvah* of *talmud Torah*, the study of Torah,[16] both as an end in itself as well as to enlighten and ennoble man, to guide us along the path of the Divinely intended human self-realization and self-perfection.

---

15. Nonetheless, it should not be surprising that there is such an effect by virtue of the comprehensively therapeutic powers of the Torah; see, e.g., *Eruvin* 54a. *Cf.* "On the Study and Propagation of *Pnimiyut Hatorah*," note 6.
16. See Rambam, *Hilchot Talmud Torah* 1:11-12; R. Shneur Zalman of Liadi, *Hilchot Talmud Torah* 1:4 and 2:1; "On the Study and Propagation of *Pnimiyut Hatorah*," note 10 and the sources cited there.

I

The Torah of G-d

The most succinct definition of Jewish mysticism is found in the *Zohar*:[17]

> *Said R. Shimon: Woe to the man who says that the Torah merely tells tales and ordinary matters.*[18] *If this were so, we could compose, even nowadays, a 'torah' dealing with ordinary matters, and an ever better one at that!*[19] *.. In reality, however, all the*

---

17. *Zohar* III:152a. See R. Mosheh Cordovero, *Or Ne'erav*, I:ch. 1-2; R. Judah Loew (*Maharal*), *Tiferet Yisrael*, ch. 13; and *cf.* R. Sholom Dov Ber (*Reshab*) of Lubavitch, *Kuntres Eitz Hachayim*, ch. 15.

18. The Torah contains many narratives, especially in the Book of Genesis (*Bereishit*), which may appear of no use or significance, as, for example, the genealogies and territories of the families descended from Noah (Genesis, ch. 10), and the genealogies of Edom (Genesis, ch. 36); *cf. Moreh Nevuchim*, III:50.

19. If the Torah were merely a history-text, a book of legends, a

words of the Torah represent lofty themes and sublime mysteries..

The Torah is clothed in 'garments' which relate to this world, because otherwise the world would not be able to contain and absorb it.[20]

The stories of the Torah are only the garment *of the Torah, as opposed to the Torah itself .. David thus said: 'Open my eyes that I may behold wondrous things out of Your Torah' (Psalms 119:18) — i.e., that which is* beneath *the garment of the Torah.*[21]

Come and see: There are garments which everyone can see. When fools see a person in clothes which to them look beautiful, they look no further..

The Torah also has a body, *namely the precepts of the*

---

practical guide for social behaviour, or some combination of these, man can easily compose a similar, and even better, work. In truth, however, the Torah is not a human or worldly composition of finite and relative value. The Torah is Divine: every word and letter is a Divine revelation to the point that a Torah-scroll in which a mistake has been made by adding or omitting even a single letter is disqualified for use as a Torah-scroll. See *Zohar* II:124a; and Ramban's Introduction to his Torah-commentary. *Cf.* R. Mosheh Cordovero, *Shi'ur Komah*, sect. XIII:ch. 44.

20. If the Torah is to be intelligible to man — a finite being living in a finite, physical world — then the Torah has to speak in the language of man (*Berachot* 31b), using anthropomorphic terminology and ideas adapted to man's mental capacity. See R. Bachya ibn Pakuda, *Chovot Halevovot*, Sha'ar Hayichud: ch. 10; and *Moreh Nevuchim* I:33. *Cf. Shi'ur Komah*, sect. LVIII; and J. I. Schochet, *Mystical Concepts in Chassidism*, ch. I.

21. *Cf.* R. Shmuel (*Maharash*) of Lubavitch, *Torat Shmuel-V:5638*, ch. 23.

Torah which are called gufei Torah *(the 'bodies', i.e., main principles of the Torah), and that* body *is vested in garments — namely the worldly tales (and language of the Torah).*

The fools of this world look at the garment, *the narrations of the Torah, and they do not know anything more. They do not consider what is beyond that garment.*

Those who realize more (than the fools) do not look at the garment *but at the* body *beneath it.*

But the wise — the servants of the Supreme King, those who stood at Mount Sinai — they look for the soul, *the very essence of everything, the real Torah. .*[22]

And in another passage[23] the *Zohar* states:

---

22. The wise see not only the outer garment and the body, but they are aware that the 'body' (the precepts; the 'letter of the law') is and must be accompanied and complemented by the 'soul' of the Torah.

　　The commentators note the seemingly parenthetical phrase 'those who stood at Mount Sinai.' They read it in context of the tradition that not only the generations of those who partook in the exodus from Egypt but *all the souls of Israel,* to the end of time, participated in the revelation and receiving of the Torah at Mount Sinai (see *Shabbat* 146a; *Pirkei deR. Eliezer,* ch. 41; *Shemot Rabba* 28:6; *Zohar* I:91a). Our text thus implies here that those who do not accept or believe that there is an inner meaning (soul) to the Torah, those who reject the mystical tradition (*sod*) — which in fact is the very essence or soul of the Torah — did not partake in the revelation at Sinai; see there R. Chaim David Azulay, *Nitzutzei Orot.*

23. *Zohar* III:149a-b.

How precious are the words of the Torah! For every single word contains sublime mysteries..

One of the thirteen exegetical rules by which the Torah is expounded states: 'When a particular case is included in a general proposition, but was then singled out from the general proposition to teach us (concerning something specific), it was not singled out to teach only concerning that specific case but to apply its teaching to the whole of the general proposition.'[24] *(Now it is likewise with the Torah itself:)*

The Torah is the supernal, general proposition. (As for the specific narratives,) however, every one of these is clearly not restricted to its very own context alone but indicates sublime ideas and sublime mysteries. 'It was not singled out to teach only concerning that specific case but to apply its teaching to the whole of the general proposition' .. that is, relating to the sublime proposition of the total Torah..

Woe to those who maintain that a particular narrative of the Torah teaches only about itself! If that were so, the supernal Torah would not be that which it really is, namely a 'Torah of Truth.'

Come and see: It is not dignified for a king of flesh and blood to engage in common talk, and less so to commit it to writing. How then can one conceive that the most high King, the Holy One, blessed be He, was short of sacred words to commit to writing and with which to compose the Torah, so that He collected all

---

24. *Sifra*, Berayta deR. Yishmael, Rule VIII.

*sorts of 'common subjects' — like the words of Esau,
the words of Hagar, the words of Laban to Jacob, the
words of Balaam and his donkey, the words of Balak,
the words of Zimri .. and the other recorded narratives, to make of them a Torah! .. No doubt but that
the supernal, holy Torah is a Torah of Truth, 'the
Torah of G-d is perfect' (Psalms 19:8), and every
single word signifies sublime matters..*[25]

This premise is so basic that Maimonides incorporated
it in the Thirteen Fundamental Principles of the Jewish
Faith, by stating: "There is no difference between verses like
'The sons of Cham were Cush and Mitzraim, Phut and
Canaan' (Genesis 10:6) or 'His wife's name was Mehatabel,
daughter of Matred' (Genesis 36:39) .. and verses like 'I am
G-d, your G-d..' (Exodus 20:2) and 'Hear, O Israel, G-d,
our G-d, G-d is One' (Deuteronomy 6:4). They are all
equally of Divine origin, and all belong to the Torah of G-d
which is perfect, pure, holy and true!"[26]

---

25. Cf. *Zohar* II:55b, and III:79b; R. Abraham bar Chiya, *Megilat
Hamegaleh* III:p. 75; *Moreh Nevuchim* III:50; R. Chaim Vital,
Eitz Chayim, Introduction. *Cf.* also Rambam's reference to
Proverbs 25:11 in the introduction to the first part of *Moreh
Nevuchim*.
26. Principles of the Faith (Commentary on *Sanhedrin*, ch. X), no.
VIII. *Cf. Zohar* I:145b; *Eliyahu Zutta*, end of ch. 2; *Shi'ur
Komah*, sect. XIII:ch. 40.

II

The Soul of the Torah

From the preceding passages of the *Zohar* we have a profound understanding of the very nature of the Torah in
general, and of its mystical dimension in particular. Jewish
mysticism, the Kabbalah and Chassidism, are *nishmata
de'orayta* (the very soul of the Torah), *pnimiyut haTorah*
(the innermost reality, the core, of the Torah), or *ma'or
shebaTorah* (the luminary aspect of the Torah which
radiates its light).[27]

The distinction between the exoteric body and the
esoteric soul of the Torah, between its external and inner
dimensions, does not imply any belittling or degradation of
the exoteric. The term *gufei Torah* implies not only body in

---

27. See *Korban Ha'edah* on *Yerushalmi, Chagigah* 1:7, *s.v.* hase'or
shebah; *Yefei Anaf* on *Eichah Rabba*, Petichta:2, *s.v.* hase'or.
Cf. below, note 45.

contradistinction to soul, but also body in the sense of substance, in the sense of 'main principles of the Torah.'[28] In this context it refers to the paramount significance of the *mitzvot*, of Halachah. Thus even those who are aware of the 'soul' of the Torah must also guard its 'body': they too are enjoined to a comprehensive study and observance of the exoteric and all its precepts. In fact, the 'body' is the very prerequisite, *sine qua non*, for attaining the 'soul.'[29]

In this context we speak of the *pardes* (orchard) of the Torah. The term *pardes* is an acronym for *peshat-remez-derush-sod*, the four dimensions of the Torah.[30] These are four dimensions of one and the same thing, thus inseparable one from the other. Even as the body is lifeless without the soul, so is the soul ineffective without the body.[31] The different dimensions thus complement one another.

---

28. See *Avot* 3:18.
29. See R. Dov Ber (*Mitteler Rebbe*) of Lubavitch, *Biurei Hazohar*, Introduction; and R. Menachem Mendel (*Tzemach Tzedek*) of Lubavitch, *Or Hatorah*, Shlach, p. 581 (especially his quotation there of R. Bachya ben Asher's commentary on Deuteronomy 29:28 citing Rambam; see also R. Bachya's *Kad Hakemach*, end of *Sukah*). Note carefully "On the Study and Propagation of *Pnimiyut Hatorah*," fn. 19.
30. In the context of the Talmudic passage of the "Four who entered the *pardes*" (*Chagigah* 14b), the *Zohar* reads the word *pardes* as an acronym for *peshat*, *remez* (or *re'iyah*), *derush*, and *sod*. These are the four dimensions, or levels of meaning and interpretation of the Torah. *Zohar Chadash*, Tikunim:107c; also *ibid.*, 102b; and *Zohar* I:26b, III:110a, and 202a. For an example of the application of these four levels of interpretation and their relationship to Chassidism, see R. Menachem M. Schneerson of Lubavitch *shelita*, *Kuntres Inyanah shel Torat Hachassidut*, ch. 9-17.
31. See above note 11. In this context note also the analogy between the esoteric dimension and salt: salt by itself is not savoury, but

On the other hand, to restrict oneself to *peshat*, to believe but in the simple, explicit meaning, is tantamount to reducing oneself to the three letters of this word, which, transposed, spell *tipesh* (a stupid person), of whom it is said (Psalms 119:70), "Their heart is *topash* (gross; dense; stupid) like fat.."[32] Even to accept *peshat, remez* (allusions) and *derush* (homiletics), but to reject or ignore the *sod* (esoterics) from *pardes*, leaves the word *pered* (mule); of him who would do so it is said (Psalms 32:9), "Like the *pered* who has no understanding..".[33]

Man cannot and may not choose and pick in matters of Torah. The Divine Torah is one entity and must be accepted as one whole. And to accept the wholeness, the oneness, of Torah, means to recognize and accept Torah on all its levels, all its facets and dimensions. This is the fundamental principle of the unity of Torah.

---

it lends savour to meat and other edibles (see *Berachot* 5a; *Menachot* 21a and Rashi *ad loc.*). It is likewise with *pnimiyut Hatorah*; see *Likutei Torah*, Vayikra, p. 3df.

32. R. Chaim David Azulay, *Midbar Kedemot*, Peh:1; and *idem, Devash Lefi*, Kof:15. See also *Shenei Luchot Haberit*, Toldot Adam (p. 3c) about the total unity of the exoteric and esoteric dimensions (citing there also Rambam's reference to Proverbs 25:11, mentioned above, note 24). *Cf.* also the Vilna Gaon's comment that knowledge of *sod* is essential for a clear understanding of *peshat*; *Even Shelemah*, VIII:21.

33. *Midbar Kedemot*, Peh:1; *Devash Lefi*, Kof:15; and *Nitzutzei Orot* on *Zohar* III:152a.

III

The "Oil of Torah"

The soul-body analogy is not just a nice metaphor. It is
meant quite literally and evokes the very nature and relevance of Jewish mysticism.

On the human level, the soul is 'unique, altogether
pure, concealed, abides in the innermost precincts of the
body yet permeates and pervades the whole body and sustains it.'[34] It is likewise with the soul and body of the Torah:
the mystical dimension is unique, concealed, altogether
pure, abides in the innermost precincts of the Torah yet
permeates and pervades its totality, and in a quite real sense
sustains it.

The Torah has been compared to various things,

---

34. *Berachot* 10a; *Midrash Tehilim* 103:4-5. See *Mystical Concepts
in Chassidism*, pp. 39-41.

including water, wine and oil.[35] All these comparisons are
not poetic devices but related to practical principles. In our
context, water, which is essential to life, signifies the Torah
as a whole. Wine and oil are liquids which are contained and
concealed within grapes and olives respectively, thus signifying the 'concealed part of the Torah,' the soul of the Torah.
The Talmud notes already that the numerical value of *yayin*
(wine) is the same as that of *sod* (secret; mystery).[36] Oil, in
turn, gives life and light to the world,[37] just as the soul to the
body.

Oil signifies distilled essence.[38] This renders it distinct
and separate from everything on the one hand, while also
pervading everything on the other. Thus oil does not mix
with other liquids: even when mixed with ever so many
liquids, it rises to the surface above them.[39] At the same
time, while other liquids remain static and will not spread
about, oil does spread itself throughout, penetrating and
pervading everything.[40]

This nature of oil is also the nature of *pnimiyut
haTorah*, the soul and mystical dimension of Torah —
shamnah shel Torah, the 'oil of the Torah.'[41] For it, too, is
essence, the essence of Torah: distinct and separate on the
one hand, yet pervasive and penetrating on the other. This is
of quite practical consequence:

---

35. *Devarim Rabba* 7:3; *Shir Rabba* on Song 1:2; and parallel
    passages noted there.
36. *Eruvin* 65a. Cf. *Zohar* III:39a and 177b; *Tikunei Zohar* 22:67a.
37. *Devarim Rabba* 7:3; *Shir Rabba* on Song 1:3.
38. On this and the next paragraph, see *Inyanah shel Torah Hachas-
    sidut*, ch. VII.
39. See references in note 37.
40. See *Chulin* 97a.
41. For this term see *Shir Rabba* on Song 1:3; and *Inyanah shel Torat
    Hachassidut*, note 48.

IV

Spiritual Schizophrenia

An exclusive study of *nigleh*, the exoteric Torah, may equip the student with Torah-knowledge. He may acquire profound scholarship. Nonetheless, it allows also the possibility that the student-scholar remain separate from the Torah itself.

On a crude level it reflects the Talmudic metaphor of the burglar who prays to G-d and invokes Divine blessing for his immoral activity.[42] That criminal believes in G-d. He believes in the principle and efficacy of prayer, yet he fails to apply that on the practical or personal level. He fails to sense the inherent contradiction in his pursuits, the radical dichotomy between his religious involvement and his personal life coexisting as two altogether separate and unrelated entities.

---

42. *Berachot* 63b, version of *Ayin Ya'akov*.

A more subtle and sophisticated dichotomy is seen in the following incident: There was a man who had studied *halachot* (the laws), *Sifre, Sifra,* and *Tossefta,* and died. R. Nachman was approached to eulogize him, but he said: "How can we eulogize him? Alas! A bag full of books has been lost!"[43]

That man had studied the most difficult texts. He had become very erudite, yet he did not comprehend and absorb what he had learned. He could quote chapter and verse, yet he and his quotations remained distinct from one another.

The *Zohar* notes that the word *chamor* (donkey) is an acronym for *'chacham mufla verav rabanan* — a wondrous scholar and a rabbis' rabbi.'[44] One can be known as the most wondrous scholar in the world, heading the most prominent academy to train rabbis and Torah-scholars, and expert in pilpulistic methodology; but if unaware of the soul of the Torah, if not touched and penetrated by the oil of the Torah, he remains an insensitive *chamor,* the proverbial "donkey loaded with books."[45] He carries a whole library on his back, has stupendous knowledge at his finger-tips, yet is not touched by what he has learned.

---

43. *Megilah* 28b, and see Rashi *ad loc.*
44. *Zohar* III:275b.
45. *Chovot Halevovot,* Avodat Elokim, ch. 4. — *Yoma* 72b provides another source for negative possibilities from an exclusive study of the exoteric part of Torah. On the other hand, a study of *pnimiyut Hatorah* (the *ma'or shebaTorah* — see above, note 27) precludes that dichotomy, because the *ma'or* of the Torah restores to the right path and goodness (*Yerushalmi, Chagigah* 1:7; *Eichah Rabba,* Petichta:2). See R. Menachem M. Schneerson of Lubavitch *shelita, Likutei Sichot,* vol. IV, pp. 1039 and 1118.

A person like that may conceivably fall to the level of a *naval bireshut haTorah* — a scoundrel and rake within the domain of Torah: he may know, observe and practice all the codified requirements of Halachah, yet be and remain a reprobate, a lowlife.[46]

Halachah is no less essential to the mystic than to anyone else. Where the Kabbalist or Chassid differs, however, is first and foremost in his approach, in his consciousness of the universal importance of Halachah and its dynamic significance. To him the study of Torah is not only a *mitzvah* on its own, or just a precondition for observing all other *mitzvot*. It is also the means to become transformed, for himself to become a Torah, a personification of Torah. One of the great Chassidic masters, R. Leib Sarah's, thus said that he traveled far and wide to come to his master, the Maggid of Mezhirech, "not to hear words of Torah from him, but to see how he laces and unlaces his shoes!"[47] He saw in the Maggid that ideal personification of Torah, where every act and motion is an expression of the ideals of the Torah.

---

46. Ramban on Leviticus 19:2.
47. See J. I. Schochet, *The Great Maggid*, p. 148.

V

Unification

To the Mekubbal or Chassid, the *mitzvot* are not only categorical imperatives of formal morality, acts of obedience and submission to G-d. The term *mitzvah* is an idiom of *tzavta*, of being joined together.[48] It implies being unified with the very act of the *mitzvah* and its contents, and thus also with the *Metzaveh*, the One Who Commanded It. Torah-study and *mitzvot* thus become the ultimate *devekut*, cleaving and attachment to G-d Himself, the *unio mystica*.

The underlying premise of mysticism is the all-inclusive exhortation of "You shall be holy,"[49] a sanctification of

---

48. R. Eleazar Azkari, *Sefer Chareidim*, Mitzvat Hateshuvah, ch. 7; *Or Hachayim* on Numbers 27:23; *Likutei Torah*, Bechukotai, p. 45c.

49. Leviticus 19:2. See Rambam, *Sefer Hamitzvot*, shoresh IV.

one's total being, of the totality of life and the world. This is a premise that precludes perfunctory study of Torah or observance of *mitzvot*, let alone being a *naval bireshut haTorah*.[50]

It is the 'oil of Torah' that penetrates, permeates and illuminates one's whole being, and transforms man and Torah into a singular entity. Every action, therefore, becomes a vital reality. This consciousness is tested and verified by the concrete realization of the premise that the purpose of wisdom is that it inspire and lead to an application of *teshuvah* (return to our Divine roots) and *ma'asim tovim* (the actual practice of good deeds).[51]

The sterile type of life and 'scholarship' of the "donkey loaded with books," unfortunately, is quite symptomatic of the modern age and its method of alleged rational inquiry, of 'logical positivism' and its atomizing games of linguistic analysis. The mystical dimension forcefully counters this and bears a pervasive message of special relevance to modern man. With this message we are able to extricate ourselves from the contemporary mind- and soul-polluting forces that threaten to stifle us, and to find ourselves. For it is the *tzinor*, the conduit connecting us to ultimate reality. It is the stimulant causing "deep to call unto deep" — the profound depth of man's soul calling unto the profound depth of the Universal Soul to find and absorb itself therein.[52] Thus it brings forth and establishes the ultimate ideal of unity, of oneness, on all levels.

---

50. See note 46.
51. *Berachot* 17a. Cf. *Likutei Torah*, Shemini Atzeret, p. 85a.
52. See Psalms 42:8, interpreted in *Sefer Halikutim al Tnach*, Toldot (p. 72) and Tissa (p. 197). Cf. *Zohar* III:73a, and *Likutei Sichot*, vol. V, p. 302.

VI

Principle of Unity

The principle of unity is fundamental to Judaism, expressing itself in each of the major concepts of our faith: G-d, Torah, and Israel.[53]

Achdut Hashem, the Unity of G-d, is a fundamental and all-comprehensive principle of Judaism, second only to existence of G-d (and in a way including that as well). We affirm it twice daily with the *mitzvah* of reciting the *Shema*, "Hear, O Israel, G-d, our G-d, G-d is One!" It implies a unique and pure oneness in an absolute sense, with nothing at all comparable to it.[54] To deny this oneness is to deny the very essence of our faith, all the precepts of the Torah, for they all depend on belief in G-d and His unity. Quite

53. See *Oti'ot deR. Akiva*-II, *s.v.* aleph (ed. Wertheimer, p. 403) that G-d, Torah, and Israel, are each referred to as "one."

54. Rambam, Principles of the Faith, no. II; and *Hilchot Yessodei Hatorah* I:7.

obviously this principle embraces also the prohibition of idolatry, the prohibition of assuming that there is any other power or reality besides G-d.[55] Idolatry is the very opposite of unity. It sets up a multiplicity of things, pluralism, realities outside and separate from G-d. Hence it is the worst sin: to believe in multiplicity is to acknowledge idolatry — which in turn is to deny the whole Torah.[56]

As G-d is the very principle of absolute unity, His creation and effects, too, manifest unity: from One can only come one.[57] Maimonides thus devotes a lengthy, and widely celebrated, chapter in *Moreh Nevuchim*, to show how the universe demonstrates in its entirety a unity like that of an individual being. Whatever differences there are between its substances are but like the differences between the limbs of a person. Just as a person is one individual, and at the same time composed of the various parts of the body (such as the flesh, bones, the various mixtures etc.), so is the universe. "This representation of the whole of the sphere as one living individual and possessing a soul .. is most necessary or useful for the demonstration that the Deity is One .. and will also clarify the principle that *He who is One has created a unitary being.*"[58]

Even as the principle of *yichud* (unity of G-d) underlies the religious life of Halachah, and *avodah zara* (idolatry) is its very antithesis, so, too, in the philosophical system of Jewish mysticism.

---

55. See *Sefer Hachinuch*, no. 420.
56. *Sifre*, Re'ey, par. 54. Rashi on Numbers 15:23, and Deuteronomy 11:28.
57. *Moreh Nevuchim* I:72. See R. Judah Loew, *Netzach Yisrael*, ch. 3.
58. *Ibid.*; see there, though, for some qualifications of the analogy. *Cf.* R. Mosheh Isserlis (Rema), *Torat Ha'olah* II:2, sect. 3.

VII

Yichud and *Perud*

Y *ichud* and *perud*, unity and division, can be said to be
the pivotal concepts of Jewish mysticism.

Yichud is at the core of everything. All being, the whole
of the creation, is as one body, the numerous members of
which are fully interrelated and interdependent. However,
just as in the analogy to the human body, the various organs
and members are bound up one in the other yet each of them
retains its own unique character and quality. Problems for
the whole, or for the part, arise where this dual nature is
ignored: when the particular shirks his universality, his
membership in, and responsibility to, the others, the whole,
and is preoccupied with himself. He commits an act of
perud, division: mutilating the universe, 'cutting down the
shoots.'

Perud, separation from the whole, in the mystic's view,

is *the* cardinal sin, the very root of all sins. Separation is caused by self-assertion, ego-centricity. It is tantamount to idolatry, creating dualism or pluralism. It is an infringement upon the ultimate *yichud*, the unity or oneness of the Absolute. For to take that stance is to establish oneself as a *yesh*, a 'something,' selfhood, a reality separate from, outside of, and next to, whatever other being there is. Thus it is a denial of the solitary unity of G-d.

The consequences of this tragic separation and division are not limited to the offending individual. The severance of a part from the whole implies not only the rejection of the whole by the part, but also the loss of the part to the whole. The whole body is rendered incomplete, deficient. It has become incapacitated with regards to the unique qualities and functions of that member. Hence the mystic's emphasis on *bitul hayesh*, the duty to negate, to efface, the ego *qua* ego, and the imperative dissolution in the whole, the concept of *devekut*, to strive for the *unio mystica*.

VIII

Bitul Hayesh

Y eshut, selfhood or self-assertion, is the very antithesis of the principle of *yichud*. It is a denial of ultimate reality vested exclusively in G-d who "fills the heaven and the earth" (Jeremiah 23:24); there is no place devoid of His presence;[59] there is none beside Him.[60]

That is why pride and anger, arrogance and losing one's temper, as well as not caring about others, and so forth, are tantamount to idolatry.[61] For in all these cases man is concerned with himself, he assumes a reality for his ego.[62] In all these cases man has become self-centered as opposed to

---

59. *Tikunei Zohar* 57:91b. See *Mystical Concepts in Chassidism*, p. 53, notes 16-17.
60. See *Mystical Concepts in Chassidism*, p. 54, note 18.
61. With reference to a) pride — see *Sotah* 4b; b) anger — see *Zohar* I:27b; Rambam, *Hilchot De'ot* 2:3; and c) not caring about others — see *Ketuvot* 68a.
62. See *Tanya*, Igeret Hakodesh, sect. XXV.

G-d-centered, worshipping his ego instead of G-d alone. He may recognize the existence of G-d, even the supremacy of G-d, but also grants recognition to himself.[63] He demands recognition for his honour, his desires, his absolute proprietorship over his possessions. At the very least this is dualism, which is no less crass idolatry than crude polytheism. This is the idolatry of which Scripture (Psalms 81:10) warns, "Let no strange god be within you."[64]

Of this self-centered person G-d says, "I and he cannot dwell together." That person is so full of himself that in him there remains no place for G-d. Of this the Baal Shem Tov taught: Self-aggrandizement is worse than sin. For of all defilements and sins it is written, "Who dwells with them in the very midst of their impurity" (Leviticus 16:16); of the arrogant, however, it is said,[65] "'I and he cannot both dwell in this world,' as it is written, 'I cannot tolerate him who has haughtiness and a proud heart' (Psalms 101:5)."[66]

Bitul Hayesh thus means total self-negation. The ego, all and any forms of selfhood, must be nullified. It has no place in the consciousness of Divine omnipresence.

To be sure, there are times and places when there is a need to demonstrate pride. Honour is due to positions of leadership, and those holding such offices must safeguard that honour.[67] No less essential is pride in one's identity as a creature of G-d, pride in one's heritage and pride in being the recipient of G-d's Torah. But that is exclusively in context of

---

63. See *Menachot* 110a; and *Tanya*, ch. 22.
64. *Shabbat* 105b.
65. *Sotah* 5a.
66. R. Ya'akov Yosef of Polnoy, *Tzafnat Pane'ach*, p. 76d (*Sefer Baal Shem Tov*, Acharei, par. 5).
67. *Cf. Kidushin* 32a-b.

the service of G-d, as it is written, "His heart was proud in the ways of G-d." (II Chronicles 17:6) It is never personalized. It is never in terms of self-aggrandizement.[68]

Bitul hayesh means conscious awareness of the ultimate nature of *adam* — man. The numerical equivalent of the term *adam* is 45, which in Hebrew consists of the two letters *mem-hey*, spelling *mah*.[69] The word *mah* means the interrogative 'what?,' signifying self-negation — as in "'What are we?' (Exodus 16:7-8), i.e., of what importance are we?"[70]

The Maggid of Mezhirech notes that the word *adam* is a compound of the letter *aleph* and the word *dam* (blood).[71] The physical reality of man is essentially *dam* (blood; the vital principle of the body). The special, metaphysical reality of man is the Divine spark that gives him life, intelligence, humanity. This Divine spark, the *neshamah* (Divine soul) is the *aleph* — from *Alupho shel Olam*, the Master of the Universe.[72] To recognize the "*Aleph — Alupho shel Olam*" as our very essence is to establish our reality as *adam* in a consciousness that *per se* we are but *mah*.[73] To forget about the *Aleph*, thus self-assertion to the point of separating the *Aleph* from ourselves, reduces us to mere *dam*, mere plasma.

68. See *Chovot Halevovot*, Sha'ar Hakeni'ah, ch. 6 and end of ch. 9. *Hilchot De'ot* 2:3. *Tzava'at Harivash*, sect. 91. *Keter Shem Tov*, sect. 68 and 393. *Tanya*, Igeret Hakodesh, sect. XXV.
69. *Tikunei Zohar*, Intr.:7b.
70. See *Keter Shem Tov*, sect. 292. Cf. *Likutei Sichot*, vol. I, Vayechi, sect. III.
71. *Maggid Devarav Leya'akov*, sect. 29; *Or Torah*, sect. 134.
72. Cf. *Oti'ot deR. Akiva*-I, s.v. aleph (ed. Wertheimer, p. 348).
73. See note 70. See also *Zohar* III:48a that *adam* is the most sublime term by which man is referred to in Scripture; and cf. R. Yosef Yitzchak (Reyatz) of Lubavitch, *Torat Hachassidut*, ch. VII; and *Likutei Sichot*, vol. IV, p. 1116, note 14.

IX

Individuality in Universality

It may appear paradoxical, but the emphasis on the universal, on the ultimate oneness of all, also emphasizes the particular. For everything created by G-d, thus everything that is part of the universal, is created for a distinct purpose, with a distinct task in relation to the whole. "All that the Holy One, blessed be He, created in His world, He created solely for His glory."[74] Every particular, therefore, is indispensable.

The toe-nails, no less than the heart and the brain, have their individual purpose: each one necessary to, and complementing, the other for the complete and perfect functioning of the body. Affectations of the toes become affectations of the brain, and vice versa. The ill-health or pain of the one affect the well-being and functioning of the other.

---

74. *Avot* 6:11.

To be sure, we do make quite clear distinctions between
them. We speak of vital and non-vital, higher and lower,
more and less important organs and limbs. We set up quali-
tative as well as quantitative scales of levels and values.
Nonetheless, they are all intertwined, interdependent, inter-
acting, with every particular adding its own contribution for
which it was created. This contribution is its very function.
To achieve it is to contribute to the well-being, the *yichud*,
of the whole. To neglect it leads to *perud*, a division and
defect in the whole.

In this context, too, it was said that everyone should
always regard the whole world as half meritorious and half
guilty. When committing a single sin, therefore, woe to him
for turning the scale of guilt against himself and against the
whole world. Thus it is said, "One sinner destroys much
good" (Ecclesiastes 9:18), that is, on account of the sin of
that individual he and the whole world lose much good. On
the other hand, if he performs one *mitzvah*, happy is he for
turning the scale of merit in his favour and in favour of the
whole world, thus bringing salvation and deliverance to
them, as it is said, "The righteous man is the foundation of
the world" (Proverbs 10:25).[75]

The significance of individuality is poignantly
expressed in the words of R. Zusya of Annapol, when he said
of his day of judgment that he did not fear the Heavenly

---

75. *Kidushin* 40b; Rambam, *Hilchot Teshuvah* 3:4. Note, though,
    that this weighing of sin against virtues is not a simple mathe-
    matical calculation. There are a number of qualitative computa-
    tions that come into play, and these are an exclusively Divine
    prerogative; see *Hilchot Teshuvah* 3:2; *Kad Hakemach*, *s.v.*
    Rosh Hashanah-I.

Judge's question as to why he had not attained the levels of the patriarchs, the prophets or even his masters; after all, who was he to compare to them? He did fear though, he said, the question of "Zusya, why were you not Zusya?"[76]

---

76. This does not contradict the principle that everyone must strive to have his deeds achieve the level of the deeds of the patriarchs (*Eliyahu Rabba*, ch. 25); for just as the patriarchs did their best to live up to their obligations and potential, so can and must every individual.

X

Cosmic Dynamics

The above now leads us to another crucial concept in Jewish mysticism: the cosmic significance of man's actions.

At the completion of *ma'aseh bereishit*, the work of creation, it is said that "G-d blessed the seventh day and made it holy, for on it He rested from all His work that He had created *la'asot*." (Genesis 2:3) It does not say there "that He had created *ve'assa* (and had made)," but the imperfect tense of *la'asot* — to make.

La'asot means *letaken* — to mend, to complete.[77] For none of the things created in the six days of creation is

---

77. *Bereishit Rabbaty* 17:1. Rashi on *Bereishit Rabba* 11:6. See R. Shneur Zalman of Liadi, *Siddur im Dach*, Sha'ar Hamilah, p. 145a; Tzemach Tzedek, *Or Hatorah*, Nitzavim, p. 1236.

complete. Whatever came into being needs further work to complete it.[78]

The world, with all its components, is incomplete. Man lacks perfection. This is not so because of some failure on the part of the Creator, nor because of some accidental defect. It is an intended part of the very plan and intent of creation. The state of incompleteness provides aim and purpose: "Which G-d has created *la'asot*" — for man to contribute, to complete himself and his share in the universe. And for that goal man was given the Torah and *mitzvot*, to sustain and complete himself and the universe.[79]

Man compounds within himself aspects of all worlds and all entities. Through his physical and spiritual composition (body and soul) he is bound up with all levels of creation. His actions and behaviour, therefore, affect all worlds, all levels, all entities, from the lowest to the most sublime.[80]

Thus the Torah repeatedly uses the phrase *ve'asitem otam* (you shall do or make them) in the context of our Divine obligations. The word *otam* (them) is usually written defective, without the vowel-sign of the letter *vav*, and therefore can be read also as *atem* (you; yourselves). Our sages see this as most significant. The implication is *ve'asitem atem* — you shall *make yourselves*, you shall create yourselves.[81]

Moreover, by observing Torah and *mitzvot* we actual-

---

78. *Bereishit Rabba* 42:3; *Vayikra Rabba* 11:7.
79. See *Tanchuma*, Shemini:7-8, and Tazri'a:5; *Bereishit Rabba* 44:1; *Vayikra Rabba* 13:3.
80. R. Chaim Vital, *Sha'arei Kedushah* III:2.
81. See *Sanhedrin* 99b; *Tanchuma*, Tavo:1; *Vayikra Rabba* 35:7.

ize their potential, we confer upon them their ultimate reality. Thus *ve'asitem otam* — it is as if you made them, the Torah and *mitzvot* themselves![82] Reaching higher yet, man's proper actions manifest the Divine reality in the world, thus leading to the daringly anthropomorphic proposition, "He who observes the *mitzvot* of the Torah and walks in His ways, it is, if it is possible to say so, as if he made Him Above. The Holy One, blessed be He, says, it is as if he has made Me."[83]

In a similar vein there is the Midrashic concept of "When Israel performs the will of the Omnipresent, they add strength to the Heavenly power, as it is written, 'To G-d we render strength' (Psalms 60:14). When Israel does not perform the will of the Omnipresent, then, if it is possible to say so, they weaken the great power of Above, as it is written, 'You did weaken the Rock that begat you' (Deuteronomy 32:18)."[84] What does that mean?

---

82. *Sanhedrin* 99b; *Vayikra Rabba* 35:7.
83. *Zohar* III:113a. See below, note 84.
84. *Eicha Rabba* 1:33; *Pessikta deR. Kahana*, sect. 26 (ed. Buber, p. 166, citing Numbers 14:17 as prooftext); *Zohar* II:32b (citing Psalms 68:35 as prooftext). For an extensive discussion of this principle, and the 'daring' concept referred to in note 83, see *Shenei Luchot Haberit*, Sha'ar Hagadol (p. 22ff.).

XI

"Partners in Creation"

Jewish mysticism uses a great deal of anthropomorphic and anthropopatic expressions. This is a major reason for the special care and caution imperative upon those who pursue it. Nonetheless, quite obviously, as with the anthropomorphisms in the Biblical and Talmudic-Midrashic writings in general, these are merely human approximations and metaphors to help finite minds understand something of the reality of the Infinite.[85]

In our context: G-d *per se* is not affected by human actions or anything else. But insofar that human actions affect the status of the universe, they determine, as it were, the flow or withholding of the Divine emanations to the universe as a whole and to each entity in particular. Man

---

85. See *Mystical Concepts in Chassidism*, ch. I.

lends the world the capacity to receive the Divine effluence. He elicits and manifests it on the level of the worlds. On the human level this is perceived as "adding strength to the Heavenly power." Conversely, man may incapacitate himself or the world from receiving the Divine effluence; thus he prevents or conceals it. On the human level this is perceived as "weakening the great power of Above."

The impact of man upon the universe, the dynamics or cosmic significance of human behaviour, the interaction between the physical and the spiritual, can be understood not only in terms of the body-metaphor (i.e., the impact of the various limbs and organs upon one another), but also in terms of the body-soul or body-mind interaction. In fact, modern technology provides phenomena that demonstrate the principle of the impact of human behaviour on an empirical level:

Radio and television show us that even the most innocuous activities of man, verily even his mere presence, leave an impression on the whole atmosphere. The voice of a man muttering to himself, and the motions of his playful jumping about, on the moon, are, by means of the right instruments, audible and visible hundreds of thousands of miles away. Sound-waves and light-rays are realities, as are atoms and various forces of energy and radiation. The science of psychiatry and psychoanalysis show how seemingly innocuous perceptions generate specific consequences, though these may not be noted until many years or decades later.

The mystic translates these facts from the phenomenal to the nouminal, from physics to metaphysics. Every activity of man, even speech and thought,[86] affects the whole cosmic

---

86. With regards to the cosmic effect of speech, see *Berachot* 19a;

order. *Mitzvot*, good deeds, proper intentions and acts, contribute to the ultimate *yichud*. Sins, evil deeds, improper behaviour, cause disorder, division, *perud*. In that sense, man, every individual, shapes and determines his own destiny and that of the world. He becomes, as it were, a partner and collaborator in *ma'aseh bereishit*[87]:

"'I have placed My words in your mouth, and with the shadow of My hand I have covered you, to plant the heavens and to lay the foundations of the earth, and to say to Zion, *ami atah*' (Isaiah 51:16) .. do not read *ami atah* (you are My *people*) but *imi atah* — you are *with Me*, to be a partner and collaborator with Me .. Just as I made heaven and earth by means of My word, as it is said, 'By the word of G-d the heavens were made' (Psalms 33:6), so do you. Happy are those who make an effort with Torah."[88]

Mo'ed Katan 18a; *Keter Shem Tov*, sect. 273; and *cf.* Responsa of *Rashba* (attributed to *Ramban*), no. 286; and Responsa *Min Hashamayim*, no. 22. For the effect of thought, see *Berachot* 60a; *Keter Shem Tov*, sect. 230 and 273; *Maggid Devarav Leya'akov*, sect. 39.

87. *Sha'arei Kedushah* III:2. Cf. *Shabbat* 10a.
88. *Zohar* I:5a. *Tikunei Zohar* 69:104a and 118a.

XII

Misplaced Humility

Man must be conscious of this immense power. He must realize that all his actions are charged with serious consequences. The Baal Shem Tov thus cautions:

> Excessive humility may cause man to go astray from the service of G-d! Because of a sense of self-deprecation he does not believe that man can bring about a Divine effluence to all worlds by means of prayer and Torah. Indeed, even the angels are sustained by virtue of man's Torah and prayers. If man would sincerely believe this, he would serve G-d with joy and gladness of the heart more than for anything else, and he would be careful with every letter, motion and word to express these in ideal fashion.

He must realize that he is a 'ladder set on the earth, and its head reaches into heaven': all his motions, his speech, his

conduct and involvements, leave impressions in the upper-
most realms. Thus he must be careful that all these be for the
sake of Heaven.

In turn, if man thinks, 'who am I that I could blemish
or correct anything above or below, that my doings will
leave a mark above' — this will cause him to follow the
inclinations of his heart, thinking that he has nothing to
worry about.

In truth, however, the good deeds of man cause him to
be literally attached to G-d, as it is written, "You shall walk
in His ways" (Deuteronomy 28:9). Thus when he is compas-
sionate below, the Supernal attribute of compassion is
stirred Above, in all worlds. This is the concept of "Know
what is Above *mimach* (from you)" (*Avot* 2:1) — i.e., from
you yourself you can know it: from the attribute aroused
within you, you know that it is likewise Above.[89]

---

89. *Keter Shem Tov*, sect. 145. See also *Tzava'at Harivash*, sect. 142,
    interpreting: "Know that what is Above — *mimcha*, i.e., it is
    from and through you." In other words, man's actions below
    determine corresponding Heavenly reactions.

XIII

Sublimation

The mystical perception of cosmic unity bridges the gap between universalism and individualism, between the universe as a whole and each person as a unique individual. There are accusations that mysticism is intrinsically antinomian. The allegation is that mystical monism erodes the reality of life, and in particular of normative Judaism with the apparent Halachic multiplicity of commandments and prohibitions categorized in terms of *issur* and *hetter* (forbidden and permitted), *kasher* and *passul* (fit and unfit), *tameh* and *tahor* (pure and impure). In truth, however, these Halachic categories can hardly emerge more clearly delineated than they do in the Kabbalah and Chassidism.

All entities are divided into the three principal groups of *chiyuv* (obligatory), *issur* (forbidden), and *reshut* (optional). In the terminology of the mystics these are: a) *Kedushah*, the realm of holiness, which embraces all that is enjoined by the Torah (*mitzvot*) and everything related thereto. b) *Sitra achara* — the 'other side,' the realm of impurity and evil, also referred to as the realm of the *kelipot* (shells; husks), which comprises all that is prohibited by the Torah and all that is related thereto. c) *Kelipat nogah* — the 'irradiated shell,' a realm related to *sitra achara* yet standing somewhere between it and *kedushah*; it includes all that is not *per se* subject to either a commandment enjoining its use or a prohibition forbidding its use.[90]

Man's relationship to *kedushah* and to *sitra achara* is self-evident: there must be active pursuit and involvement with all in the realm of *kedushah*, and conscious passivity and abstention with regards to all in the realm of the *sitra achara*. When thus relating to them, in their Divinely intended context, they both serve their purpose and achieve their ends: holiness is strengthened, absorbed and diffused, and evil is subdued and nullified, in the world as a whole and in the individual involved in particular.

The real test of life relates to the vast realm of *kelipat nogah*, which is both profane and neutral. It is profane because of its present status as, and association with, *kelipah*. It is neutral, because its *nogah* — its irradiation from the side of *kedushah* — partly neutralizes its bond with *kelipah* to the point of allowing it to be a realm of potentiality. It is the not-yet-hallowed even as it is the not-yet-defiled. It is potential *kedushah*, even as it is potential *sitra achara*. Whether it will be sublimated to ascend to the one, or degraded to descend to the other, depends on how it is used by man.

---

90. For an extensive discussion of this subject, see *Mystical Concepts in Chassidism*, chapters X-XI.

One and the same piece of skin may become sacred parchment of a Torah-scroll, or an evil cat-o'-nine-tails to torture and abuse; the same coin may serve to save someone in need, even as it can also be used for bribery and corruption. Thus it is with the myriads of daily activities of professional involvements, business-conduct, eating, drinking, sleeping, walking, talking, and all the (permissible) objects and tools related to these.

XIV

Involvement *vs.* Asceticism

T he concept of sublimating the mundane, of actualizing the potential of the not-yet-holy (or to use the terminology of mysticism: of extricating and liberating the sparks of Divine holiness inherent in all created entities[91]), means active involvement.

Man is a compound of body and soul, placed in a material world. The Divine soul of man *per se* is not in need of *tikun* (mending) at all,[92] and there was no need for it to be vested in matter and the world except to draw G-dliness into *them*, to mend *them*.[93] The material body and material objects are mended and sublimated by means of the Torah

---

91. See *Mystical Concepts in Chassidism*, ch. VII, p. 134*ff*.
92. R. Chaim Vital, *Eitz Chayim* 26:1.
93. See *Tanya*, ch. 37.

and *mitzvot* which the soul performs with their aid. The literal and figurative descent of the Divine soul from its sublime source to a gross, material world, therefore, is to mend the world, to elevate it to become absorbed in pure *kedushah*, and the achievement of this sublimation elevates the soul itself as well. But, again, this purpose of creation implies direct involvement, to use everything in this world as Divinely ordained.

This goal excludes an approach of asceticism. Asceticism — self-denial, fasting, self-mortification — can and does serve a valid purpose, but only within certain boundaries. *Yechidei segulah*, a select few individuals of high spiritual stature, are able to achieve the Divine intent through asceticism just as others do through a normative way of life.[94] Many great mystics, including large numbers of the Chassidic masters who publicly spoke out against asceticism and discouraged their followers from pursuing it, were themselves strict ascetics. There is a legitimate and recommended asceticism even for people of lower stature, as in the context of *teshuvah* (whether on the level of *teshuvat hamishkal* — to do penance for sins committed, or of *teshuvat hageder* — as precautionary measures in the face of personal weaknesses).[95] Generally speaking, though, asceticism is negativism, escapism.

The ascetic individual (beyond the exceptions mentioned) opts out: he evades reality, he avoids involvement,

---

94. See *Chovot Halevovot*, Sha'ar HaPerishut, ch. 1-2. Rambam, *Shemonah Perakim*, ch. 4.

95. See *Tzava'at Harivash*, sect. 56 and 78-79, and see there the sources cited in my notes. *Cf.* Rambam, *Shemonah Perakim*, ch. 4; *Hilchot De'ot.* ch. 4; *Hilchot Nedarim* 13:23.

adhering but to the minimal essentials for bare survival. He practically rejects the realm of *kelipat nogah*, scared off by seeing only its negative side, the evil-in-potency. Moreover, self-mortification weakens and reduces man's energy. "A worker may not famish or chastise himself because this would cause him to lessen from his work."[96] This applies no less to the work and labour of life, to the service of G-d.[97] Self-denial of the legitimate and permissible, therefore, though undertaken with good intentions, may still be tantamount to sin.[98]

The mystic does not lose sight of the danger inherent in the raw-material of the mundane, but his perspective causes him to cast his eyes upwards: he sees the not-yet-hallowed, he is conscious of the Divine sparks hidden in the not-yet-consecrated. Thus he will not withdraw. He contemplates the world as Divine creation, the Divine omnipresence, the aspects of Divinity within himself and within the world around him. He chooses, nay, he feels compelled to adopt the road of involvement, regardless and in spite of it being

---

96. *Yerushalmi, Demay* 7:3; Rambam, *Hilchot Sechirut* 13:6.
97. *Ta'anit* 11b; *Shulchan Aruch*, Orach Chayim, sect. 571. *Cf.* R. Judah Halevi, *Kuzari* III:1-5.
98. *Ta'anit* 11a. See *Tanya*, Igeret Hateshuvah, ch. 3. *Cf. Radvaz* on Rambam, *Hilchot Sanhedrin* 18:6, that man's body is not his private possession but the exclusive property of G-d. This leads to the significant ruling stated in *Shulchan Aruch Harav, Choshen Mishpat*, Hilchot Nizkei Guf Vanefesh, par. 4, that the human being has no authority over his own body to smite or to shame it, or to afflict it in any manner of affliction — even by withholding some food or drink (unless for a legal and truly beneficial purpose)! For an extensive discussion of this principle, see Rabbi S. Y. Zevin, *LeOr Hahalachah* (Tel Aviv 1964), p. 318*ff*.

more difficult and more tortuous. He feels compelled to actualize, expose and manifest the latent "for My glory I have created it, formed it, and made it."(Isaiah 43:7) For he realizes that without this, the universal body is deficient, as every particular creature is essential for the completion and perfection of the whole in its Divinely intended context.[99]

The sublimation and transformation of *kelipat nogah*

---

99. Here apply Rambam's words, that "In this context I have never heard a more remarkable statement than that in the Jerusalem Talmud, in the ninth chapter of *Nedarim* (9:1) .. Rav Idi said in the name of R. Yitzchak, 'Is what the Torah has forbidden not enough for you that you prohibit yourself yet other things as well?';" *Shemonah Perakim*, ch. 4; see *Hilchot De'ot* 3:1. *Cf.* also *Yerushalmi, Kidushin*, end of 4:12.

Needless to say, this is not a license for self-indulgence, but applies only in context of "Let all your deeds be for the sake of Heaven" (*Avot* 2:12) and "Know Him in all your ways" (Proverbs 3:6; see below, end of sect. XVIII), as stated by Rambam *ad loc. cit.*, and see commentaries on *Yerushalmi, Kidushin* 4:12. In all other cases, when a person's present status renders him unable to achieve the sublimation and sanctification of *reshut* (the optional), it is obligatory to set up fences to safeguard the inviolability of the Torah (*Avot* 1:1; *Yevamot* 21a). The rule is to "sanctify yourself in that which is permitted to you" (*Yevamot* 20a; *Sifre*, Re'ey, par. 49; see *Pessikta Zutraty*, preamble to Kedoshim). All the qualifications of the sources cited above, notes 94-95, apply, in the spirit of the Chassidic aphorism that "whatever is forbidden is forbidden, and that which is allowed is unnecessary" (*Likutei Sichot*, vol. I, Noach, end of sect. V). Ethical texts thus caution that it takes restrictive measures in seventy areas of the permissible and optional in order to avoid trespassing the boundaries of a single area of the prohibited (*Chovot Halevovot*, Sha'ar Hateshuvah, ch. 5; *cf. Or Hachayim* on Numbers 26:23). For a discussion of these premises see *Likutei Sichot*, vol. I, Acharei, and *ibid.*, Kedoshim, sect. VI-XIII.

is an act of redemption. It redeems not only the particular object used, but also the agent using it. For the human body and its vital or 'animal' soul, too, are of the realm of *kelipat nogah*,[100] and the actualization of their potential of holiness is their very purpose. This individual redemption, bringing "redemption to my soul" (Psalms 69:19), is a prelude to the universal redemption.[101] For it contributes to the ultimate goal of total *yichud*, the goal towards which everything strives, when "In that day G-d shall be One and His Name shall be One." (Zechariah 14:9)

100. See *Tanya*, ch. 1 and 7.
101. See the Baal Shem Tov's interpretation of Psalms 69:19 in *Toldot Ya'akov Yossef*, Shemini:1, and *ibid.*, Devarim:1 (*Sefer Baal Shem Tov*, Shemot, par. 5-6, and note 4 *ad loc.*).

XV

"In *All* Your Ways.."

The *Mishnah* teaches: "Who is strong? He who subdues his *yetzer* (evil disposition)."[102] The Baal Shem Tov notes that it does not say "he who breaks; tears asunder and destroys," but "subdues." One does not need too much strength or skill to 'break' the *yetzer*, but well to 'subdue' it. To subdue it means to control it, to control and utilize the energy and power of the *yetzer* for sacred purposes, as it is said, "There is much increase with the strength of the ox (euphemism for the *yetzer* and the 'animal soul')" (Proverbs 14:4).

He offers a parable: A man once heard a robber trying to break into his store. Thus he cried loudly for others to come and help him defend his property, and the robber ran away. Another man had the same thing happen to himself,

---

102. *Avot* 4:1.

but he kept silent: he waited for the thief to enter, and caught him. He did not want to scare the robber away, lest he return another time and succeed. This is the meaning of conquering and subduing.[103]

In the same context, the Baal Shem Tov offers an original homily on the verse, "When you see the *chamor* (donkey) of your enemy lying under its burden, you might want to refrain from helping him, but you must surely help him" (Exodus 23:5):

"When you see the *chamor*," that is, when you consider your *chomer*, your material reality,[104] i.e., the body, you will note that it is "your enemy;" for it hates the soul which craves G-dliness and spirituality. Moreover, you will also note that it is "lying under its burden," i.e., the yoke of Torah and *mitzvot*. For the Holy One, blessed be He, placed the yoke of Torah and *mitzvot* upon the body so that it become purified and sublimated by it, but the body regards this as an unwanted burden. Thus one may think to "refrain from helping him;" that is, one might consider that the way to fulfill our mission is to adopt fasts and self-mortifications to crush the body and break its matter. The verse, therefore, concludes that this is not the way to cause the light of Torah to reside; rather, "you must surely help him": purify and refine the body, and do not crush it by mortification.[105]

A story is told of the Maggid of Mezhirech: Friday-

---

103. *Keter Shem Tov*, Hossafot: par. 91; *cf. ibid.*, sect. 171.
104. The letters of *chamor* are the same as those of *chomer*, rendering these two words interchangeable. See R. Judah Loew, *Gevurot Hashem*, ch. 29; *Torah Shelemah* on Exodus 4:20, note 109; *Tzava'at Harivash*, sect. 100.
105. *Keter Shem Tov*, Hossafot:16. *Cf. Degel Machaneh Ephrayim*, Mishpatim (cited in *Sefer Baal Shem Tov*, Mishpatim, par. 8).

afternoons he would retire to his room to rest. One Friday he sent his attending student to stop one of his great disciples, R. Aaron of Karlin, from reciting *Shir Hashirim* (Song of Songs, customarily read by many on the eve of Shabbat). The Maggid stated that R. Aaron's recital aroused and stormed all supernal worlds, and thus prevents him from sleeping. Many understood the point of this story to be the greatness of R. Aaron and the sublimity of his worship. A great Chassidic sage, R. Hillel of Paritsh, however, saw it different. He said that the moral of the story is the greatness of the Maggid: quite evidently his sleeping was still more sublime, a still greater form of worship, than R. Aaron's recital of *Shir Hashirim*; for otherwise he would not have stopped him!

This is the principle of "Know (acknowledge) Him in *all* your ways" (Proverbs 3:6) which the Talmud regards as the "brief passage upon which depend all the fundamentals of the Torah."[106] It means to know and acknowledge G-d in our physical involvements and preoccupations no less than in our blatantly spiritual ones.[107] It means to recognize the underlying *yichud* and interaction of all, and the implicit cosmic significance of everything we do. The Baal Shem Tov, in his interpretation of this verse,[108] emphasizes the word *da'eyhu* (Know Him), which has the connotation of joining together, of unifying.[109] The implication is to use 'all your ways,' even the physical and material involvements, to further, bring about or effect, *yichud*, ultimate unity.

---

106. *Berachot* 63a.
107. See *Hilchot De'ot* 3:3.
108. *Tzava'at Harivash*, sect. 94; *Keter Shem Tov*, sect. 282. See also *Keter Shem Tov*, sect. 217 and 236; and *Maggid Devarav Leya'akov*, sect. 131, 256, and 259.
109. See *Tikunei Zohar* 69:99a; *Tanya*, ch. 3.

XVI

G-d-Consciousness

The concept of Divine Omnipresence, of the pervasiveness of G-dliness, implies also the concept of *hashgachah peratit* — of Divine Providence relating to every detail of all creatures and entities in the world and universe.[110]

The principle of *hashgachah peratit* is itself charged with significant consequences. For it infuses not only the obligation to seek and recognize Providential intent in all one sees, hears and experiences,[111] but also moulds the very consciousness of man in general. It confers the power of

---

110. See *Keter Shem Tov*, sect. 427, and *ibid*. Hossafot, sect. 63, 101, 121-2, and 125. See also next note.
111. See *Keter Shem Tov*, sect. 46, 220; and *ibid*. Hossafot, sect. 123-4, and 126-9. *Maggid Devarav Leya'akov*, sect. 69, 213, and 238. *Or Torah*, sect. 107, 115, 314, and 317.

positive thinking, an attitude of optimism and joy, and inspires an activist approach to man's service of G-d.

To be sure, G-d's presence is hidden, vested and concealed in many 'garments.' Nonetheless, the very knowledge of this, the awareness of the reality of Divine Omnipresence, the consciousness that the whole earth is full of His glory and that every motion and thought originates in Him, this in effect removes the screens of G-d's hiddenness and 'causes all workers of iniquity to be scattered.'[112] Thus everyone must realize that he is never ever forlorn: wherever he may be or go, G-d is always with him.[113]

"One must forever keep in mind the Creator's omnipresence, and that His *Shechinah* is with you at all times .. One must always be joyful, keeping in mind and believing with absolute faith that the *Shechinah* is with him and guards him; he is bound up with the Creator, and the Creator is bound up with him in all his limbs and faculties. He 'looks' upon the Creator, and the Creator looks upon him. All good things as well as judgments in the world are rooted in G-d, for His effluence and vitality are in everything; thus 'I trust but in Him, and fear but Him, blessed be He.'"[114]

In short, "*Shiviti Hashem* — I have set G-d before me at all times; as He is at my right hand, I shall not falter" (Psalms 16:8). That is, 'I acknowledge and sense the Omnipresence of G-d, that G-d is all and that all is in G-d.'[115] Moreover, *shiviti* has a double meaning. The principle of

---

112. *Keter Shem Tov*, sect. 51 and 85.
113. *Keter Shem Tov*, Hossafot, sect. 136.
114. *Tzava'at Harivash*, sect. 137; and see also *ibid.*, sect. 84.
115. See the quotations from the writings of R. Mosheh Cordovero in *The Great Maggid*, p. 70f.

setting the Divine Presence and Providence before us at all times, per force implies also the interpretation of *shiviti* as an idiom of *shaveh* (equal), thus rendering the concept of equanimity: 'everything is equal to me;' there is personal indifference to any affectations to the ego (the concept of *bitul hayesh*), because 'G-d is before me at all times.'[116]

---

116. *Tzava'at Harivash*, sect. 2; and see there the sources cited in the notes.

XVII

Positivism *vs.* Negativism

The *yetzer hara* (evil disposition) in man seeks to weaken this consciousness. It tries to convince man that his imperfections or sins disqualify him from any bond with G-d. The *yetzer hara* thus strives to make man feel depressed and despondent, in order to make him think that his service of G-d is unacceptable and futile.

Feelings of *atzvut* (depression) over our status and assumed sinfulness may appear motivated by spirituality, by honest introspection. In truth, however, they result but from the seductive wiles of the *yetzer hara* trying to prevent man from serving G-d and performing *mitzvot*. The excessive self-deprecation underlying those feelings are but a subtle form of self-assertion, a disguised obsession with the ego: "I am no good! Of what value or significance would or could be *my* deeds. Any involvement with Torah and *mitzvot* on my part would be tantamount to hypocrisy." This attitude then serves as a conscious or subconscious excuse to move in the opposite direction of crude self-indulgence.[117]

To be sure, there is nothing wrong with feelings of regret and contrition, with self-deprecation. The principle of *teshuvah*, of repentance for improprieties and a return to G-d, demands these. But the authenticity and sincerity of such feelings, to discover whether they derive from the *yetzer tov* or the *yetzer hara*, is tested by their consequences: if they lead to self-improvement, to an intensified attachment to G-d and Torah, they are good; if not, they are clearly from the *sitra achara*.

Atzvut — melancholy, depression — is rooted in evil, in egotism, regardless how noble the accompanying thoughts may appear.[118] Here, again, enters the concept of *bitul hayesh*. For regardless of a person's status, regardless of whatever he may have done in the past, when it comes to serve G-d, to observe Torah and *mitzvot*, he must say to himself: "Never mind myself! The service of G-d is not for *my* sake, but to fulfill the will of G-d. While I must indeed do *teshuvah*, nonetheless, right now I must forget all about myself and do that which the Almighty wants me to do!"[119] In the words of the Maggid:

"Turn away from evil and do good" (Psalms 34:15). When it comes to matters of Torah and *mitzvot*, it is incumbent upon man to repel any thoughts of 'Who do you think you are, you lowly creature! You have done such and such, thus how dare you presume to enter the inner sanctum

---

117. See "Serve G-d With Joy," sect. I-II.
118. *Ibid.*, sect. II.
119. *Tzava'at Harivash*, sect. 44 and 46.

of Divine service!' One must realize that such thoughts are but the wiles of the *yetzer hara* waylaying him to harm him and to make him neglect his service. Scripture thus advises: "*Turn away from evil*" — i.e., from those thoughts that remind you of your evil deeds, and "*Do good.*" Do not allow any weakening of your service, but rise to pursue it as if you had never done any wrong.[120]

This *bitul hayesh*, rooted in the consciousness of Divine omnipresence and *hashgachah peratit*, with their implicit cause for faith, trust and joy in G-d on the one hand, and the realization of the cosmic significance of man's behaviour on the other hand, leads of itself to a rectification of that which is in need of mending. Thus it prevents any going astray.

Pnimiyut haTorah penetrates and transcends the body and garments of material reality, the evil and darkness that

---

120. R. Ze'ev Wolf of Zhitomir, *Or Hame'ir*, Shabbat Teshuvah. *Cf.* R. Israel ibn Al'Nakawa, *Menorat Hamaor*, Perek Hamitzvot (p. 394f.; also appended to *Reshit Chochmah*): "A person must never think and say to himself, 'I am a sinner and have committed many iniquities, thus of what use would it be for me to observe *mitzvot*' (*cf. Shabat* 31b; *Kohelet Rabba* 7:17). On the contrary: if he committed many transgressions then he should now perform many *mitzvot* against these. Thus it is stated in *Vayikra Rabba* (21:5) in comment on (Proverbs 24:6), 'Conduct your war with *tachbulot* (discerning steering)': if you have committed bundles (*chabilot*) of transgressions, counteract them by performing corresponding bundles and bundles of *mitzvot* .. and as the Midrash notes that man should make an effort to perform *mitzvot* with the very same limb which he used for sinning.."

See also *Sefer Chareidim*, Mitzvat Teshuvah, ch. 4: "Though a person may be depressed because of his sins, he must be joyful in the service of G-d .." *Cf. The Great Maggid*, pp. 191-3.

appear to the physical eye. It does so by emphasizing, seeking and unveiling the good and the positive, the soul and light, in everything.[121] Evil is overcome by doing good, by redeeming the Divine sparks inherent in everything, and not by direct or indirect involvement with the evil itself. For 'he who wrestles with a filthy person is bound to become soiled himself.'[122] The proper approach, then, is to follow the old proverb that "even a little bit of light banishes a great deal of darkness" of itself and by itself.[123] Hence the emphasis on optimism, on *bitachon* (trust in G-d) and *simchah* (joyfulness),[124] and on the principle that "the actual deed (of Torah and *mitzvot*) is the most essential thing."[125]

---

121. *Cf. Torat Hachassidut*, ch. 11*ff*.
122. See *Tanya*, ch. 28.
123. R. Bachya ibn Pakuda, *Chovot Halevovot*, Sha'ar Yichud Hama'aseh, ch. 5; R. Nissim Gerondi, *Derashot Haran*: V (p. 70); *Tanya*, ch. 12. See below, p. 117, note 4.
124. See *Reishit Chochmah*, Sha'ar Ho'ahavah, ch. 12 (cited in "Serve G-d With Joy," sect. III, and see there note 26).
125. *Avot* 1:17; *Tikunei Zohar* 52:87a; *ibid.* 60:93b, and 70:133b*f*.

XVIII

Redemption

The Messianic age is typified by a universal manifestation of G-dliness: "The earth shall be full of the
knowledge of G-d, as the waters cover the sea" (Isaiah 11:9),
when it shall no longer be necessary for "every man to teach
his fellow.. for they shall all know Me, from the least of
them unto the greatest of them" (Jeremiah 31:33).[126] This
means a transcending of the present-time empiricism, to
penetrate to the hidden reality concealed by the veneer of the
physical and sensual world of appearance. It is a time when
G-d will "yet appear unto them once more to explain the
mystery of the Torah's reasons and the secrets of its hidden
treasures."[127]

---

126. *Zohar* III:23a; Rambam, *Hilchot Teshuvah* 9:2, and *Hilchot
Melachim* 12:4-5.
127. Rashi on Song 1:2.

In other words, it is a time when *pnimiyut haTorah*, the soul of the Torah, will be revealed and manifest.[128] The opportunity to have a glimpse and taste of that time, however, exists already now.

A study and pursuit of *pnimiyut haTorah*, to the extent that it is readily available, especially in the teachings of the Baal Shem Tov and his disciples, affords the opportunity to transcend the frustrating restrictions and perplexing constraints of our present-day reality of *galut* and a world steeped in materialism with its consequences of egocentricity and subsequent inhumanity and suffering. This transcendence is achieved by absorbing and internalizing the perspective of the mystical dimension of the Torah. It is the perspective of spirit over matter, of soul over body, of absolute reality over transient appearances.

With this perspective man achieves personal redemption and a transcendence of *galut* in all its meanings. This, in turn, leads to the ultimate Messianic redemption for the world at large. For the sole difference between *golah* (exile; diaspora) and *ge'ulah* (redemption) is the single letter *aleph*[129] — signifying *Alupho shel Olam*, the Master of the Universe: inserting the *Aleph* into *golah*, the conscious recognition, awareness and acting upon the presence of *Alupho shel Olam* even in *golah*, brings of itself *ge'ulah* — when the illusory veil concealing the Face of G-d shall be removed and "the glory of G-d shall be revealed so that (even) all flesh shall see.." (Isaiah 40:5) in a truly empirical way.[130]

---

128. See *Kohelet Rabba* 11:8. Cf. *Tanchuma*, Tavo:4.
129. R. Shmuel (*Maharash*) of Lubavitch, *Mayim Rabim — 5636*, ch. 134. Cf. *Netzach Yisrael*, ch. 1.
130. See *Likutei Sichot*, vol. XV, p. 44.

Jewish Mysticism:
Authentic Tradition
vs. Subjective Intuitions

Jewish Mysticism: Authentic Tradition *vs.* Subjective Intuitions

Table of Contents

Jewish Mysticism:
Authentic Tradition
vs. Subjective Intuitions

I

Mysticism

Mysticism. The word itself mystifies. It excites feelings of awe and anticipation: an indefinable awe and dread in the awareness of forbidding depths beyond the normative reach of man; yet also anticipation of discovering secrets that confound even as they arouse curiosity.

Man is defined as the rational being. To be rational means to think, and to think means to be inquisitive, to search. Our search encompasses questions about our very being — our source of origin and our ultimate destiny; questions about the meaning of life, the purpose of existence.

Oftentimes we embrace quick answers so that our search may come to rest in some certitude. Yet again and again our certainties are shaken. Some try to escape by denying their doubts. They submerge themselves in social and professional ambitions and identities. Yet moments of spontaneous reflection recur. Thoughts touching issues that transcend the here-and-now force themselves upon us again and again.

Every so often we snatch a glimpse of that transcendence. It may come in a state of contemplation. It may come from a deeply touching experience: from an experience of consummate love, from a perception of the immensity of nature, from being transported to ecstasy by music or poetry, or from so many other experiences that penetrate the very core of our being.

Such glimpses are part of what we call mystical experiences. They are not restricted to a select circle of initiates to the esoteric sciences, nor to those who have withdrawn from the mundane. The mystical experience, in the wide sense of the term, is an integral part of the human experience. It is native to all people, without distinction of race or creed. With some more, with others less — yet, universal.

The universality of mysticism is both fascinating and problematic. It has made mysticism the subject of academic study and scientific research — to be analyzed, classified and categorized by professionals in the fields of theology, philosophy and psychology. For the mark of mysticism is not only the intense feeling of the mystical experience, but also, and more so, its effects.

Nothing is closer to man than an actual experience. The more gripping — the more real it is to him. Thus it is not surprising that a mystical experience causes man to draw practical conclusions affecting his philosophical perspective and judgments.

Obviously, these conclusions are relative to the experience, to the degree of its intensity and its perceived relevance. They are also relative to the individual's mind and emotions. In other words, these conclusions are highly subjective. They may differ drastically one from the other, even contradicting one another. They are influenced by many varying factors: personal background, previous commitments or inclinations; they are colored by mental and psychological conditioning.

II

The Mystical Experience

This leads to our basic problem: how authentic is the experience? How reliable are the "vibrations" and how valid are the conclusions? How and where do we draw the line between the authentic and the spurious, between the reliable and the deceptive, the true and the imagined, the valid and the specious?

William James, a well-known philosopher and psychologist, summarized four distinguishing marks of the mystical experience:

(a) Ineffability: it defies expression. That is, no adequate report of its content can be given in words. Its quality must be experienced directly: mystical states are more states of feeling than states of intellect.

(b) Noetic quality: the mystical experience appears to the subject as a state of knowledge, an insight into the depths of truth that are unplumbed by the discursive intellect. It is an illumination, indeed a "revelation," full of significance and importance, inarticulate though it remains.

(c) Transiency: it cannot be sustained for long.

(d) Passivity: it "hits" the subject, grasping and holding him like a power beyond him, beyond his control, as if his own will is in abeyance. To be sure, the experience can be induced by voluntary operations as, for example, fixing attention (meditation), bodily performances (e.g., yoga exercises), or intoxicants (alcohol, drugs) that will stimulate the mystical consciousness. Certain aspects of nature may awaken mystical moods. Nonetheless, in the actual experience of the "event," for the "contents" of the experience, the subject is in effect passive.

The most powerful aspect of the mystical experience is clearly the innate feeling that everything is charged with meaning. The subject feels surrounded by "truths" which he is as yet unable to grasp, but they arouse indescribable awe. He is filled with cosmic consciousness, a consciousness of the life and order of the universe. He senses an intellectual enlightenment that leads him to new planes of existence. There is moral exaltation, an indescribable feeling of elation, a quickening of the moral sense — as striking and more important than the enhanced power of the intellect.

Moreover, mystical states, when developed, are usually authoritative for the individual who experiences them; he "has been there" and just "knows."

Here lies both the fascination and the problem, the beauty and the fundamental weakness of mysticism and mystical experiences.

III

The Dilemma:
Conservatism *vs.* Anarchy

Many have already observed that mysticism may move man into various and varying directions: some to conservatism, others to revolution; some to deeper commitments, others to anarchy and nihilism.

For some the experience is a rediscovery of self, enhancing and reinforcing their personal, social or religious identity by lending it deeper meaning, new dimensions. Others again are led to a radical reinterpretation of their philosophical or religious systems, often to an allegorical spiritualization of the external forms and dictates of their tradition. For many it is the conscious or subconscious excuse for a self-indulgent anti-nomianism in which the experience, the personal "turn-on," is the standard and the goal. It does not matter to them whether the experience is a striking flash of intuition from without, or whether it is induced from within by the mechanical means of auto-suggestion, meditation or drugs.

An historical review of mystics and mystical schools, in the East and in the West, within our Jewish tradition and outside of it, readily offers evidence of these trends.

We are familiar with giants of the spirit who were intoxicated by their insights and experiences to a renunciation of the self. They were moved to forgo all pursuits of the ego and submerged themselves in the ultimate reality of omnipresent Divinity to become a vehicle for the Will of G-d.

We know also of movements and individuals who intoxicated themselves to reach altered states of consciousness for their self-indulgence, and used their illusions to justify excesses of all sorts.

This polarity is reflected in the very nature of mysticism. For mysticism is by definition monistic and pantheistic. There are, though, two kinds of pantheism:

(a) There is a physiomonistic pantheism which identifies the world, the physical realm, the here-and-now, as the sole reality: the "I, man, world, nature" is the centre of all — indeed, is all. Good and evil, therefore, are not distinguishable in any absolute sense; they are but in the eye of the beholder.

(b) There is a theomonistic pantheism which recognizes G-d alone as the ultimate reality: "there is nought but He alone." "I, man, world, nature" — these have no reality of their own and exist solely by virtue of the Creator's Will. This is not simply pantheism, but panentheism: G-d is in all; all is in G-d; G-d is all. The world is not a place that contains Him, but He contains the world. His Will, therefore, is the criterion for right and wrong, good and evil. There are absolute values.

This brings us back to our problem: How and where do
we draw the line between authenticity and self-delusion? Are
there objective standards to serve as guidelines, or must we
find our own way in a chaotic jungle of subjective feelings
and relative insights? Are mystical schools just different fads
or forms of cults — some of which appear acceptable
because (generally speaking) they conform to basic social
and philosophical standards, while others are rejected
because they contravene conventional norms?

As for Jewish mysticism: is it just one other school, just
one more facet, in the wide spectrum of mysticism? Is it
distinguished from all others merely by its particular religious label, but otherwise essentially the same?

Before trying to answer these questions we must first
define the term "cult," especially in its presently negative
connotation of "extravagant and faddish attachment to a
person or system of worship or ritual."

IV

What Is A 'Cult'?

I would define "cult" as any form of faith or belief that is based on an unfounded commitment: a "blind belief," a "blind leap of faith." To be sure, the believer may be altogether sincere. The doctrines or teachings espoused may appear altogether noble. The objectives may seem idealistic and commendable. Nonetheless, if the commitment is based on purely personal feelings and emotions, if it is devoid of any rational foundation and lacks valid "reasons for the belief" (be they historical or philosophical), then we have no choice but to condemn it as a cult.

This definition applies to any form of theological or philosophical system that is charged with practical consequences; i.e., that would commit its adherents to adopt a distinct way of life and practices.

To determine who would fall into this category one may simply ask: "Why do you follow or accept your belief?"

If the answer contains:

(i) a reason that is more or less defensible from a logical point of view; or

(ii) a reason (or form of reasoning) that the proponent would consider or respect when presented to him in defense of a view differing from (or opposing) his own, then he has shown fair justification for himself.

To be sure, in the latter case he need not necessarily accept the conclusions derived from the other's premises. He may have equally good or better reasons to move into an altogether different direction; but he can at least understand and appreciate the other position — "it does make some sense."

If, however, the premises and conclusions can be shown to be blatantly untrue or invalid; if the reasoning is inconsistent and logically untenable; if the proponent would not accept his own kind of "reasoning" and "proof" when offered by another to justify a radically different or opposite approach, and just stubbornly proclaims: "Just believe! Just accept!" — then he is shown to be self-serving, senseless, acting out of ignorance and/or pure emotionalism. He is not reasoning but rationalizing. He is not in pursuit of truth but of self-justification. He is mentally blind; irrational; in effect — dishonest. His system is no better than the worst he would condemn in others.

This yardstick must be applied to the realm of religion more than anywhere else. For religion is by definition all-encompassing; comprehensive. When speaking of G-d and religion we are dealing with ultimate truth, the most important thing in life.

We are not talking about transient values, momentary gains, about "take-it-or-leave-it" propositions. We are not involved with wagers, taking chances.

To the believer, religion is everything. It relates to his soul, as opposed to his body. It relates to salvation, as opposed to comforts. It relates to eternity, as opposed to the here-and-now. It relates to absolute truth, as opposed to pragmatism or efficiency.

When it comes to buying a used car, or even the simple purchase of a common item, we make the effort to investigate, to evaluate, to consider carefully that the article is worth the surrender of our money. We all know the relative value of money, and that the loss of even a substantial sum is not an insurmountable tragedy. Yet we go out of our way to protect this transient property.

When it comes to obtaining medical advice, even of a non-vital nature, we make the effort to investigate, to evaluate, to consider carefully, that the doctor is a reliable and conscientious authority. In more serious cases, as for an operation — even when there are no life-threatening consequences — we go out of our way to obtain a second opinion, preferably the opinion of specialists in the field.

Anyone in his right mind goes out of his way to protect his physical well-being and comfort, and to insure his worldly property and possessions — notwithstanding the fact that these are but transient, here-and-now, and can be protected only up to a certain limit and degree. How much more so then, must we be careful, critical and investigative when it comes to matters of religion — matters of spiritual well-being, salvation, eternity! There is no greater absurdity than to be more careful with the mundane, with matters relating to our body and money, than in matters relating to our soul and salvation.

This is the absurdity — indeed insanity and outright self-contradiction — of blind commitments, blind leaps of faith. This is not faith but credulity. This is not "conversion" but seduction. This is not "rebirth" but suicide. It reduces religion to a level far inferior to anything mundane.

A rational person would not buy something just because of its external attractiveness, or because of the charm or oral promises of the salesman. How much less so can or should we accept philosphical or theological premises just because of the emotional magnetism of their external attractiveness and the promised dreams of those soliciting.

We all remember Jim Jones and his Jonestown. We all know horror-stories of youngsters (and elderly) involved with the many other cults of gurus and evangelists. The trouble, though, is that most people recognize the harm and absurdity of those cults because they are so different from our conventional norms — yet fail to ask themselves whether they are really different in principle; whether their own approach to the ultimate issues is different in essence; whether they themselves are not also seduced and brainwashed by emotional magnets, by the allurements of the world or society around them, by values and practices whose meaningfulness and benefits are but relative to a present time and location.

This applies to our approach to G-d and religion in general, and to our personal practices in particular. This applies to the way that many of us seek to mold and shape our religious or ethical principles and practices to our likes and caprices, instead of molding and shaping our likes and caprices to the ultimate dictates and practices of our religion.

An excellent example of this definition and description of "cult" can be found in a very bizarre source. At the murder trial of the notorious Manson-"family" in California, one of the defendants addressed the jury before sentencing: "What I did came from the heart, from love. Whatever comes from the heart and flows out of love cannot be evil. You cannot stand in judgment over me...!"

This emotionalism, this centrality of the heart, this obsession with self — that is the ultimate sign of a cult, the distinctive mark of the crudest of all idolatries: self-worship. True religion deals with the question: "What does G-d require of man?" False religion, a cult, deals with the question: "What does man expect from G-d?"

V

The Uniqueness of Jewish Mysticism

We can now return to the earlier questions. The line can and must be drawn in the context of an honest, objective and critical self-evaluation. The line can and must be drawn in the context of a frank and open pursuit of truth, regardless of what the consequences may be; without prejudging, without personal bias, without considering what others might think or say. We need no more than the same criteria used in determining our general concept of truth and reality — the same criteria, be they historical or philosophical; no more.

It is here that Jewish mysticism differs radically from all other kinds or schools of mysticism.

Judaism is based on the public Revelation at Sinai, when the Torah was given to Israel. The historical event of

Sinai attests to the Divine source and nature of the Torah, and the Torah in turn serves as the exclusive criterion for any subsequent claims and teachings.

Authentic Jewish mysticism is an integral part of Torah, and Torah determines what is authentic Jewish mysticism.

The general term for Jewish mysticism is *Kabbalah*. *Kabbalah* means tradition. The *Kabbalah* is not a compound of personal insights. It is not a collection of reports of what various sages and saints had to say on the meaning of life and ultimate values — based on their mystical experiences or visions. It is not a system born in a vacuum.

The *Kabbalah* and its teachings — no less than the *Halachah* — are an integral part of Torah. They are traced back to the historical roots of Sinai, part and parcel of "*Mosheh kibel Torah miSinai umesarah...* (Moses received the Torah from Sinai and transmitted it...)."

To be sure, in various works of the *Kabbalah* one can find reports of mystical experiences, visions, the supernatural — all those things and more which we normally link to mysticism. They are there, but they are not the essence or even a major part of the *Kabbalah*. At best they are effects, possibilities or potential effects, that may accompany a mystic's life. The authentic mystic, however, will not seek to manipulate, and will shun interfering with the natural order instituted by the Creator.

The authentic mystic seeks knowledge, understanding. He wants to "Know the G-d of your father," to fulfill the precept of "You shall know this day and consider in your heart that G-d He is G-d in Heaven above and upon the earth below — there is nothing else." He seeks to realize and understand this axiom not only as an intellectual affirmation of truth but as a living reality within the limits of his capacity — profoundly sensing the literal omnipresence of G-d, with a penetrating understanding and knowledge, as much as possible.

VI

The Authenticity of *Kabbalah*

K abbalah is theology in the fullest sense — including ontology, cosmogony and cosmology. It is not speculative philosophy based on human insight nor theories derived from human reasoning. It is a study, as it were, of Divinity and of the relationship between G-d and His Creation, based on the premises of revealed truth.

The *Kabbalah* takes man beyond the normative understanding of reason. It goes beyond the exoteric part of Torah and transcends normative existence. It uncovers many of the infinite layers of the secrets of life, of Creation, of the soul, of the heavenly spheres. It penetrates beyond the garments and the body of the Torah. It is the very core and soul of Torah, the ultimate revelation of Divinity — exposing the inner meaning, effects and purpose of Torah and *mitzvot*. The illumination emanating from the *Kabbalah* ignites the soul of man, setting it on fire in the awareness of a deeper and higher reality. Its study and insights are themselves mystical experiences. The *Kabbalah* is all this — but always and exclusively within the context of Torah. As a body cannot function without a soul, so the soul is ineffective without the body. The soul of the Torah (*nistar*, the esoteric part of the Torah) can never be separated from the body of the Torah (*nigleh*, the exoteric parts; *Halachah*, the commandments and practices prescribed by the Torah). *Kabbalah* reduced to spiritual or philosophical symbolism, stripped from the observance of the *mitzvot*, is worthless mumbo-jumbo, an empty shell.

This is the first and foremost difference between Jewish mysticism and all other kinds and forms. That is why Jewish mysticism can never fall into the category of a cult.

The great mystics and philosophers outside Judaism, in the East and in the West, were honest and sincere sages. They did seek truth. They did not look for answers to justify or verify any of their preconceived notions. They were not indulging their egos. And many did discover and develop profound theories and insights which stir the imagination and move the human spirit. Some had glimpses of ultimate reality. Yet, in spite of all this, they worked in a chameleonic void. They could move only as far as finite and fallible man is able to reach on his own. Their insights or findings, therefore, are either humanly verifiable (that is, logically self-evident truth or tautologies) or else speculative truth which at best contains an element of possibility but never the assurance of certitude.

The *Kabbalah*, on the other hand, builds on the revealed truth of Torah. The validity of its speculative theories and subjective experiences must be, and *is*, tested and verified by that truth in order to be worthy of consideration, to be viable and acceptable. It has, and continually uses, objective criteria to make it consistent with, and as reliable as, *Halachah*.

VII

Conclusion

At this point, though, we must realize that Jewish mysticism — the *Kabbalah* and Chassidism — is not just a legitimate and respectable part and dimension of authentic Judaism, of Torah.

The Torah is an organism, a complete whole in which every part is most intimately interrelated and interwoven with every other part; in which everything is interdependent upon everything else. The Torah is an organism analogous and parallel to, and in complete interaction with, the organism of the universe in general and the organism of man in particular. No part or particle, therefore, can be taken in isolation from the others.

Thus, even as it is incumbent upon each and every one of us to pursue the study and practice of the "body" of the Torah — *Halachah*; *mitzvot* — so it is obligatory and essential for each and every one of us to pursue the study and inspiration of the "soul" and fruits of the *Torah* and its interpretation.

To be sure, each of us is limited by his or her natural capacities. No one can absorb the totality of the Torah in its Divine infinity. But everyone can and must actualize his or her own potential, can and must reach out as far as his or her abilities can take them.

In fact, nowadays more than ever before, there is a most urgent need for the illumination and inspiration of the mystical dimension of the Torah. This very need is the great vision and contribution of the Baal Shem Tov and Chassidism. This very need is the purpose of this evening and the purpose of all the events of our "Symposium on Jewish Mysticism."

These events were not meant to be another series of lectures for intellectual stimulation and academic knowledge. If they do not lead to practical consequences, if they will not inspire practical results and enhance spiritual and moral consciousness, then they may very well have been a waste of time.

The purpose of it all is to become linked with the Ultimate Essence, even if only in some small way. For essence is indivisible, and as the Baal Shem Tov taught: "When you grasp even a part of essence, you are holding all of it!"

❋   ❋   ❋

Rabbi Zusya of Annapol, one of the great masters of Chassidism, said: "When my day comes and I will stand before the Heavenly Throne of Judgment, I shall be asked: 'Zusya! Why were you not as good and great as the patriarchs — Abraham, Isaac and Jacob?'

"But I shall not be scared by that question. I will answer quite simply: 'How can I be compared to them? I am but a simple person without any special qualities. The Patriarchs were holy men, like unto angels, endowed with sublime souls. There is no comparison whatsoever. The question is altogether unfair!'

"The same answer will apply to any other comparison with ancient or recent saints. I do not fear questions like these. One thing, though, I am very much afraid of and have no excuse for, namely, when I shall be asked: 'Zusya, why were you not Zusya?'"

We are not asked to ascend into the high heavens nor to traverse the wide seas. We are not asked to become what we are not. All we are asked to do is to be ourselves: to be true to ourselves; to actualize our own true nature, our own abilities, our individual missions in life.

This is what it is all about, and the rest is but commentary. So now let us go forth and study — "to comprehend and to discern, to perceive, to learn and to teach, to observe, to practice and to fulfill all the teachings of G-d's *Torah* with love."

"Let Your Wellsprings Be Dispersed Abroad":

On The Study And Propagation Of *Pnimiyut haTorah*

"Let Your Wellsprings Be Dispersed Abroad":

On the Study and Propagation of *Pnimiyut haTorah*

Table of Contents

"Let Your Wellsprings Be Dispersed Abroad":

On The Study And Propagation Of *Pnimiyut haTorah*

*On the Day of Judgment, when the Holy One, bless-
ed be He, shall judge the whole world in the Valley of
Yehoshaphat .. the Holy One, blessed be He, shall say
(to man): 'My son .. did you look into the* Merkavah?
*Did you look into the Sublime? For there is no greater
delight in My world but the time that the students of
the wise sit and busy themselves with the words of
Torah, and gaze, look, see and dwell on the abun-
dance in this study: about My Throne of Glory...'*
Midrash Mishlei, ch. 10

I

"The *Neshamah* Hears!"

On several occasions when discussing mystical concepts
of the Kabbalah and Chassidism with my father and

teacher זללה"ה, he would recall an interesting incident. His first master, Rabbi Joseph Leib Bloch — rabbi and *rosh yeshivah* of my father's native Telz — often referred to Kabbalistic concepts in his ethical discourses. When the rabbi was challenged that these ideas are alien to his listeners, and often difficult to understand, he would reply: "The *neshamah* (soul) understands!"

This reply was not a cavalier retort. It harbours a profound thought discussed in Chassidism and articulated a century earlier by R. Dov Ber of Lubavitch (the *Mitteler Rebbe* — 5534-5588; 1773-1827), as seen in the following episode.

The famed Chassidic sage Rabbi Hillel of Paritsh was delegated by R. Dov Ber to visit numerous towns and villages. He was to collect funds to redeem coreligionists who had been incarcerated and for other charitable purposes. At the same time Rabbi Hillel was to encourage and strengthen the religious life of the communities he visited, and he reviewed for them Chassidic discourses he had learned in Lubavitch. The people he met on his travels ranged from the scholarly and perceptive to the quite simple, and this fact raised some doubts in Rabbi Hillel's mind. He asked R. Dov Ber whether to continue reviewing Chassidic discourses for those unable to understand them. The *Rebbe* answered in the affirmative and said:

> "The teachings of Chassidism are heard by the *neshamah* (soul). Scripture states, 'And flowing streams from *Levanon* (Lebanon)':[1] *Levanon* stands

---

1. Song 4:15. *Cf.* R. Shneur Zalman of Liadi, *Likutei Torah*, Ha'azinu, p. 71d; *ibid.*, Shir, p. 5d.

for *Lamed-Bet* [and] *Nun*,[2] i.e., the *Chochmah* (wisdom) and *Binah* (understanding) in the *neshamah*.[3] When the *neshamah* hears, there is a flow and stream in the illumination of the soul which vivifies the body, and this results in a strengthening of the *asey tov* (do good)[4] relating to the 248 commandments [which the Torah enjoins man] to do, and of the *sur mera* (turn away from evil)[4] relating to the 365 prohibitions [of the Torah]."[5]

2. The word *Levanon* is divisible into two components, each forming a symbolic number: the first two letters (*lamed-bet*) form the number 32, alluding to the '32 wondrous paths of *chochmah*' (*Sefer Yetzirah* 1:1; *cf.* R. Mosheh Cordovero, *Pardes Rimonim* 12:1*ff.*); and the remaining three letters spell *nun*, the letter equivalent to the number 50 and alluding to the '50 gates of *binah*' (*Rosh Hashanah* 21b; *Zohar* I:4a and 261b). See R. Menachem Mendel (*Tzemach Tzedek*) of Lubavitch, *Or Hatorah-Nevi'im*, vol. I, p. 373.

3. *Cf.* R. Levi Yitzchak Schneerson, *Likutei Levi Yitzchak-Zohar*, vol. II, p. 183 (on *Zohar* III:16a). The author notes there also that *Balevanon* has the same numerical equivalent as *chochmah-binah*.

4. Psalms 34:15: "*Sur mera* — turn away from evil, *ve'asey tov* — and do good." Chassidism emphasizes that after an initial cognizance to avoid wrong-doing (see *Tanya*, ch. 41; also *ibid.*, ch. 31) man's essential concentration and involvement should be with the positive aspect of *asey tov*. This will then of itself effect the negative *sur mera*, just as the kindling of light dispels darkness. See *Likutei Torah*, Shir, p. 48b-c; and R. Menachem M. Schneerson of Lubavitch, *Likutei Sichot*, vol. I, p. 124*f.*; vol. II, p. 473*f.*; vol. V, p. 460*f.* *Cf.* the Baal Shem Tov's comment that the light of Torah (goodness) causes darkness (evil) to disappear, in *Degel Machaneh Ephrayim*, Nitzavim; see *The Great Maggid*, ch. XII; and "To Be One With The One," ch. XVII.

5. R. Menachem M. Schneerson of Lubavitch, *Hayom Yom*, p. 31. *Cf.* the comment of R. Shmuel (*Maharash*) of Lubavitch cited in *Sefer Hasichot 5700*, p. 138.

II

Universal Relevance

The difficult and complex concepts and doctrines of Jewish Mysticism are all-pervasive in Chassidism. This fact, however, must not deter either the teaching or the learning of it. There is a unique merit, an objectively purifying, edifying and invigorating effect, in the very perusal of these sacred texts, as with Torah in general,[6] even if they are difficult to understand and sometimes not comprehended.[7]

---

6. Cf. *Kidushin* 30b; *Eliyahu Rabba*, end of ch. 6 (on *Menachot* 5:8), *ibid.*, ch. 18 (on Lamentations 2:19), and ch. 21 (on Numbers 24:5); *Eliyahu Zutta*, end of ch. 9; *Tikunei Zohar* XXI:49a; *Tzava'at Harivash*, sect. 29 and 51, and the notes *ad loc.*; *et passim.*

7. See R. Mosheh Cordovero, *Or Ne'erav* V:2; R. Chaim Yosef David Azulay, *Avodat Hakodesh, s.v.* Moreh Ba'etzba 2:44; and below, note 29. See also R. Yechezkel Landau (*Noda Biyehudah*), end of Foreword to *Tziyun Lanefesh Chayah* (*Tzlach*), on *Berachot* (citing R. Noach of Brody).

This objective and independent potency makes it possible for all to become involved with *Pnimiyut haTorah* (the "inner" aspects of the Torah). The significance thereof is far-reaching, in view of the fact that the precept of *Talmud Torah* (Torah-study) is all-comprehensive, demanding that each and everyone study Torah to the best of his abilities and the utmost of his capacities — on all four levels of the Torah:[8] *Peshat* (simple meaning), *Remez* (allusion), *Derush* (hermeneutics), and *Sod* (esoterics; mysticism).[9] The *possibility* of involvement with *Pnimiyut haTorah*, therefore, implies of itself *obligation* of involvement.[10]

The advent of R. Israel Baal Shem Tov, who revealed

Cf. *Avodah Zara* 19a, and *Tossafot, ibid.*, 22b; *Zohar* I:185a, and III:85b; *Sefer Chassidim*, sect. 1164, and *Mekor Chessed, ad loc.; Likutim Yekarim*, sect. 3; and R. Shneur Zalman of Liadi, *Hilchot Talmud Torah* 2:13.

8. See *Shulchan Aruch Arizal, s.v.* Keri'ah Bechochmat Hakabbalah; R. Chaim Vital, *Sha'ar Hagilgulim* XVI-XVII; *idem, Sha'ar Hamitzvot*, Introduction; *Hilchot Talmud Torah* 1:4 and 2:10.

9. In the context of the Talmudic passage (*Chagigah* 14b) of the "Four who entered the *pardes* (garden; orchard)," the *Zohar* (*Zohar Chadash*, Tikunim:107c) reads the word *pardes* as an acronym for *peshat, remez* (or *re'iyah*), *derush* and *sod* — which signify the four dimensions or levels of interpretation of the Torah. See "To Be One With The One," note 30.

10. See *Hilchot Talmud Torah, ad loc.* (above, notes 6 and 8), and also 2:2. Cf. R. Chaim Vital, *Sha'ar Ru'ach Hakodesh*, p. 108b; *Tanya*, Igeret Hakodesh, sect. XXVI. See also *Aruch Hashulchan*, Yoreh De'ah 246:15.

Note the comment of R. Eliyahu, the Vilna Gaon, on *Midrash Mishlei*, ch. 10 (quoted above), that the obligation to study *Pnimiyut haTorah* applies even to the wicked whose conduct is far removed from the Torah-way of life; *Even Shelemah* 8:24, and note 20 there. See *Likutei Sichot*, vol. IV, p. 1039f.

and disseminated *Pnimiyut haTorah* in the form and modes
of *Darkey haChassidut* (the ways and practices of Chassidism) and *Torat haChassidut* (the teachings of Chassidism),
lent special impetus to the aforementioned. In the famous
epistle addressed to his brother-in-law, R. Abraham Ger-
shon of Kotov,[11] the Baal Shem Tov recalls a wondrous
experience:

> "On *Rosh Hashanah* 5507 (1746) I performed the
> evocation of *aliyat haneshamah* (ascent of the soul to
> celestial spheres) ... I saw wondrous things in a vision
> as I had not seen heretofore since the day I reached
> maturity. It is impossible to relate and tell, even face
> to face, what I saw and learned when I ascended
> there.
>
> "...I ascended level after level until I reached the
> palace of the Messiah, where the Messiah studies
> Torah with all the *Tannaim* (teachers of the *Mish-
> nah*) and the *Tzadikim* (righteous people), and also
> the Seven Shepherds[12] ... I asked the Messiah: 'When
> will the master come [to redeem Israel]?' And he
> answered:
>
> *"By this you shall know it: when your teachings will*

---

11. This letter was published by R. Ya'akov Yosef of Polnoy (to
    whom it had been entrusted by the Baal Shem Tov for delivery to
    R. Abraham Gershon), as an appendix to his *Ben Porat Yosef*.
    Subsequently it has been reprinted in whole or in part in *Keter
    Shem Tov* and other works. *Cf. The Great Maggid*, p. 115; and
    Shivchei Habaal Shem Tov, ed. Y. Mundshein, p. 229*ff*.

12. Adam, Seth, Methuselah, Abraham, Jacob, Moses and David;
    see *Sukah* 52b, and *Shir Rabba* 8:9. *Cf.* the gloss by *Tzemach
    Tzedek* in *Likutei Torah*, Beha'alotecha, p. 33b, and his *Or
    Hatorah-Nevi'im*, vol. I, p. 476*ff*.

*become renowned and will be revealed throughout
the world, and 'your wellsprings will be dispersed*
chutzah *(abroad; externally)'* (Proverbs 5:16) ... then
the kelipot[13] *will perish and it will be a time of
propitiousness and deliverance.'...*"[14]

R. Moshe Chaim Ephraim of Sudylkov, the Baal Shem
Tov's grandson and disciple, refers to this letter in his
writings and adds:

"This [reply of the Messiah] seems alluded in the verse
'And the children of Israel went out [of Egypt] *beyad ramah*
(with uplifted hand; Exodus 14:8). [*Targum Onkelos* renders the translation of *beyad ramah* as] *bereish galey* (openly).
Bereish is an acronym for *R. Israel Baal Shem,* and the word
galey alludes to the time when his teachings shall be revealed
and his wellsprings will be dispersed; that is when [Israel]
shall come out of exile."[15]

---

13. *Kelipot* (shells; bark) is the mystical term for the aspects of evil;
    see *Mystical Concepts in Chassidism,* ch. 10.
14. *Keter Shem Tov,* sect. 1 (p. 2a-b). For a Chassidic interpretation
    of this encounter see R. Yosef Yitzchak of Lubavitch, *Likutei
    Diburim,* vol. II, sect. 16-18 (esp. pp. 572 and 618*ff.*).
15. *Degel Machaneh Ephrayim,* Beshalach. See *Likutei Sichot,* vol.
    III, p. 872*f.*

III

Change in Status

The Baal Shem Tov's vision in essence reflects an ancient premise of the mystics, as stated in the *Zohar*:

> " 'And they that are wise shall shine as the splendor of the firmament' (Daniel 12:3) with this work of [R. Shimon bar Yochai], i.e., the Book of the Zohar (Book of Splendor) ... And because in the future Israel will taste from the Tree of Life,[16] the Sefer

---

16. In Kabbalistic terminology, the 'Tree of Knowledge of Good and Evil' (Genesis 2:9) symbolizes the exoteric Talmud and Halachah (which deal with the clarification of what is permitted, fit and pure, and what is forbidden, unfit and impure; in other words, the clarification or 'knowledge' of 'good' and 'evil'), and the 'Tree of Life' symbolizes the esoteric dimension of the Torah, the Kabbalah. See the sequel of our passage in the *Zohar* (and its interpretation in *Igeret Hakodesh*, sect. XXVI),

haZohar, *they will leave the exile with it, in mercy.*"[17]

".... *And so many people here below (on earth) shall be sustained* (yitparnessun) *by this work of [R. Shimon bar Yochai] when it will be revealed in the last generation, at the end of days, and in the merit thereof 'You shall proclaim liberty throughout the land' (Leviticus 25:10).*"[18]

The teachings of the Kabbalah originally were restricted to *yechidei segulah*, a chosen few whose saintliness matched their scholarship and who had mastered the strict prerequisites[19] to entering the orchard of mysticism. "The

---

and *Zohar Chadash*, Tikunim:106c-d. *Cf.* also *Zohar* III:153a; and R. Sholom Dov Ber (*Reshab*) of Lubavitch, *Kuntres Eitz Hachayim*, ch. 3, 5, 11-13, and Appendix III.

17. *Zohar* III:124b, explained at length in *Igeret Hakodesh*, sect. XXVI.

18. *Tikunei Zohar* VI:23b-24a. See also *ibid.* XXI:53b (and the commentary *Kissei Melech, ad loc.; cf. Zohar* III:153b); and *Zohar Chadash*, Tikunim:96c.

19. See *Zohar Chadash*, Bereishit:6d: "One must not reveal the mysteries of the Torah except to a person that is wise and studied Scripture and Talmud, whose studies endure, and he is G-d-fearing and erudite in everything." *Cf. Chagigah* 11b and 13a; Rambam, *Hilchot Yessodei Hatorah* 4:13; *Zohar* III:105b, and 244a (and *Nitzutzei Orot*, and *Nitzutzei Zohar, ad loc.*); and below, note 20.

   R. Mosheh Cordovero notes that he who wishes to pursue the esoteric teachings of the Torah must first possess some basic knowledge of *nigleh* (the exoteric Torah), the laws relevant to the daily life of the Jew. Otherwise he would be like one who "gazes at the stars, only observing the things above him, and thus failing to see holes right under his feet; ultimately he will

whole science of the Kabbalah had been concealed from all
the scholars except for a select few — and even that was in a
mode of 'walking secretly' and not publicly, as mentioned in
the *Gemara*.[20] ...R. Shimon bar Yochai, too, stated in the
sacred *Zohar*[21] that permission to reveal was given to him
and his associates only."[22] This concealment and restriction,
however, was to last only to 'the end of days,' i.e., to the
period immediately preceding the Messianic era.

"The decree against open involvement with *Choch-
math haEmeth* (the Wisdom of the Truth, i.e., the Kabbalah) was but for a set period of time, namely up until the
end of the year 5250 (1490). From then onwards it is called
the 'last generation,' and the decree was nullified and it is

---

fall into a deep pit." *Or Ne'erav*, I:ch. 6. *Cf.* Rambam, *Moreh
Nevuchim* I:33-34, and also *ibid.*, ch. 31-32.

To study the mysteries of the Torah before Scripture, Mishnah and Talmud is at best "like a soul without a body, lacking
efficacy and accountability.. Man must study the wisdom of the
Kabbalah, but first his body must be purified. This is effected by
practicing the *mitzvot* — which serve this purpose (*cf. Bereishit
Rabba* 44:1) and are essential. Only thereafter can the *neshamah*
(soul) — 'The soul of man is a lamp of G-d' (Proverbs 20:27) —
radiate in this body like a lamp placed in a glass reflector:
shining and invigorating him to understand the mysteries of the
Torah and revealing its depths..;" R. Chaim Vital, Introduction to *Eitz Chayim*.

See also Ramban's introduction to his commentary on the
Torah; the strict words of caution of the Baal Shem Tov quoted
in *Keter Shem Tov*, Hossafot, sect. 26 (and the notes there); and
R. Dov Ber of Mezhirech, *Or Torah*, sect. 258. *Cf.* also *The
Great Maggid*, p. 116, note 17.

20. See *Pesachim* 119a; *Chagigah* 11b and 13a; *Kidushin* 71a.
21. See *Zohar* III:159a; also *ibid.*, II:149a and III:79a; *Tikunei
Zohar* Intr.:1a.
22. *Igeret Hakodesh*, sect. XXVI.

permissible to occupy oneself with the *Zohar*. Since the year 5300 it is a most meritorious precept to be occupied therewith in public, for both the great and the small. As it is by virtue of this merit, and not another, that the King Messiah will come in the future, it is improper to be slothful [with this study]."[23]

Indeed, in this context R. Shimon bar Yochai foresaw an ever-increasing revelation of mysticism in the period preceding the Messianic redemption to the point that "when the days of the Messiah will be near at hand even young children will happen to find the secrets of wisdom."[24]

---

23. R. Abraham Azulay, quoting earlier sages, in his introduction to *Or Hachamah*.
24. *Zohar* I:118a. Cf. Rashi's commentary on Song 1:2; and Rambam's reference to the restoration of prophecy prior to the Messianic redemption, in *Igeret Teyman*, ed. Kapach, p. 49 (see also *Moreh Nevuchim* II:end of ch. 36). Cf. *Likutei Sichot*, vol. II, p. 588*f*.

IV

"*Mitzvah* to Reveal"!

The century following the year 5250 — referred to above — witnessed a phenomenal flourishing and revolutionary expansion in the study of, and preoccupation with, the Kabbalah. It was the age of R. Mosheh Cordovero, whose expository works — of remarkably lucid style — have become primary sources. Immediately after him followed R. Isaac Luria, the *Ari* ("Lion"), whose all-encompassing teachings soon were recognized universally as final and authoritative and had an impact on the totality of Jewish life.[25] It was an age that ushered in an altogether new era: R.

---

25. See R. Joseph Ergas, *Shomer Emunim* I:17.

For the basic difference between the systems of R. Mosheh Cordovero and R. Isaac Luria, see R. Chaim Vital, *Sefer Hachizyonot* II:17; R. Mosheh Zacuto's glosses on *Eitz Chayim* and *Mevo She'arim*, note 2 (appended to *Mevo She'arim*, ed. Tel

Isaac Luria declared that as of then it is not only *permissible* but a *mitzvah*, a *duty*, to reveal *Pnimiyut haTorah*, the esoteric part of Torah.[26]

Ever since then there has been a continuous flow of mystic works appearing in print: the writings and teachings of the aforementioned R. Mosheh Cordovero and R. Isaac Luria, and of their disciples; commentaries on the *Zohar*; mystical expositions of the Bible and Rabbinic texts; special tracts propagating the principles and premises of the Kabbalah and introducing the novice to them. All these works, mostly written by scholars whose authoritative expertise in the Talmudic-Halachic branches of the Torah equalled their mastery of the Kabbalah, stressed the significance of, and

---

Aviv 1961, p. 335a); R. Menachem Azaryah de Fano, *Pelach Harimon*, end of Introduction. (See also *Sefer Toldot Ha'ari*, Jerusalem 1967, sect. VI, p. 158*f.*; and *cf. ibid.*, p. 100, note 1, and p. 178*f.*)

26. *Igeret Hakodesh*, sect. XXVI. See R. Chaim Vital, *Sefer Hagilgulim*, ch. 32: "In this our present era, which is the last era, it is necessary to reveal *chochmat Ha'emet* (lit. 'the wisdom of Truth'; the mystical teachings of the Torah) in order that Mashiach will come, as stated in *Tikunei (Zohar)* that by merit of the *Zohar* the King Mashiach will be revealed."

See also R. Chaim Vital, *Sha'ar Hahakdamot*, Introduction; *Kuntres Eitz Hachayim*, ch. 13, 21, and Appendix III; *Kuntres Inyanah shel Torat Hachassidut*, Appendix; *Likutei Sichot*, vol. VII, p. 206*ff.*

On the obligatory aspect of the study of *Pnimiyut haTorah* see also *Tanya*, Kuntres Acharon, sect. IV (p. 156b); the quotation of R. Shmuel (*Maharash*) of Lubavitch, in *Sefer Hatoldot-Maharash*, p. 81; R. Yosef Yitzchak (*Reyatz*) of Lubavitch, *Kuntres Limud Hachassidut*, ch. 10; and *Or Hachassidut*, p. 169*ff.*

need for, an intensive study of *Pnimiyut haTorah*[27] — the

---

27. See especially R. Isaac ben Immanuel de Lattes' approbation for
the first printing of the *Zohar* (prefacing most editions since
then); R. Mosheh Cordovero, *Or Ne'erav* (parts I-V); *Sha'ar
Hahakdamot*, Introduction; *Or Hachamah*, Introduction; *Shomer Emunim*; and so forth. These, and many others, went to
great lengths to refute in detail the various objections raised to
an extensive study of mysticism. They state emphatically the
admissibility and necessity thereof nowadays, in spite — and
precisely *because of* — the spiritual decline of our own times (see
below, ch. IX-X).

Note also R. Chaim Vital's resolution of the seeming contradiction between this claim on the one hand and the restrictive
prerequisites referred to above (notes 19-21) on the other, by
stating: "If we were to apply the prerequisites as strictly as they
appear to be, no one would be able to pursue this study unless he
had an instructor as great as R. Shimon bar Yochai to resolve all
problems encountered. Thus it seems to me that the *mitzvah* to
pursue this wisdom remains in effect, provided one has adopted
the following approach: when seeing bewildering passages
which may arouse doubts, one must think 'If this matter appears
to be in vain — it is on *my* account (see *Sifre*, Ekev, end of par.
48; *Yerushalmi*, *Pe'ah*, 1:1; *cf.* "To Be One With The One,"
note 12); that is, I do not understand it because of the deficiency
of *my* intellect, and not, Heaven forbid, because the subject-
matter is questionable'.. The study (of mysticism) is prohibited
only to him who is unable to stand in the Palace of the King and
may come to heresy, Heaven forbid, because he thinks himself
very wise and without any deficiency on his part;" *Kol Ramah*
on *Zohar* III:141a (quoted in *Nitzutzei Zohar*, *ad loc.*); also *Eitz
Chayim*, end of Introductions. Cf. *Moreh Nevuchim* I:ch. 31-
34, and *ibid.*, III:ch. 26 and 50.

See further the sources cited in preceding note; the frequent
discussion of this theme in *Likutei Sichot* (see there index, *s.v.*
Hafotzat Hama'ayanot; Chassidut; Pnimiyut Hatorah); and the
anthology *Or Hachassidut*.

very soul[28] of the Torah which animates and illuminates the body of the exoteric tradition.[29]

However, this open dissemination of the Kabbalah, which began gradually in mediaeval times and expanded drastically from the sixteenth century onward, remained restricted basically to the scholarly world. Two centuries passed since R. Isaac Luria before there was a further development bringing the *Zohar's* vision of the 'end of days' a major step closer to realization.

---

28. The exoteric and esoteric components of the Torah are usually compared to, and referred to as, the 'body' and the 'soul' of the Torah; see *Zohar* III:152a; *Sha'ar Hahakdamot*, Introduction; *Kuntres Eitz Hachayim*, ch. 15. (See "To Be One With The One," ch. I-II) *Cf.* Rambam's distinction between *nigleh* (the revealed, exoteric) and *nistar* (the concealed, esoteric) parts of the Torah, comparing them to silver and gold respectively; *Moreh Nevuchim*, Introduction (in comment on Proverbs 25:11).

29. On the illuminating aspect of *Pnimiyut haTorah* in relation to the other parts of the Torah, see *Or Ne'erav*, parts IV-V; *Kuntres Eitz Hachayim*, ch. 21ff.; *Kuntres Torat Hachassidut*; *Kuntres Limud Hachassidut*; and *Kuntres Inyanah Shel Torat Hachassidut*.

V

Advent of Chassidism

A new era began with the rise of R. Israel Baal Shem Tov who revealed and propagated the teachings of Chassidism.[30] In this new stage mysticism was popularized on a much wider scale. Chassidism made it possible that not only the discerning scholar but *every one* may 'taste from the Tree of Life' and be inspired by it.

The Baal Shem Tov propagated and disseminated ideas and ideals of *Pnimiyut haTorah* in such ways and manners as could be absorbed by all, by each relative to his own level. During his numerous travels he would address differing

---

30. See R. Chaim ibn Atar, *Or Hachayim* on Leviticus 6:2, and *ibid.* on Numbers 26:22, that the "morning of the manifestation" would follow with the year 5500 (which coincides with the period of the Baal Shem Tov and the beginning of the Chassidic movement). *Cf. Migdal Oz*, ed. J. Mundshein, p. 495*f.*

audiences with short and seemingly simple comments or parables relating to Torah and the Divine service. His pithy words were easily understood by simple folks at whom they were often directed and set their souls on fire to worship the Omnipresent with renewed vigor and enthusiasm. His words, however, invariably were based on, and contained and alluded to, profound premises and insights of the mystical depths of Torah. His scholarly disciples, too, therefore, could and would probe these teachings and meditate on them to extricate their inexhaustible lessons relating to themselves at their own level of scholarship and understanding.[31]

This new approach, of an extensive study of *Pnimiyut haTorah*, continued in one form or another through the second generation of Chassidism, led by R. Dov Ber of Mezhirech,[32] and those following thereafter. Every attempt was made to realize fully the 'dissemination of the wellsprings of Chassidism *chutzah*' — outside, i.e., even in such places and to such people which at first glance might seem far removed from any relationship with the subject-matters of Chassidism.[33] If at first this dissemination had been indirectly, or in a transcendent mode of 'the *neshamah* hears and understands,' this, too, was to change in the course of time.

---

31. See *Degel Machaneh Ephrayim*, Vayeshev, and *ibid.*, Tetzaveh (Likutim); *Likutei Sichot*, vol. III, pp. 874-5.
32. See *The Great Maggid*, ch. VII.
33. See *Likutei Sichot*, vol. I, p. 316; vol. III, pp. 873 and 1006; vol. IV, p. 1119*f.*; vol. V, pp. 364 and 432*f.* Cf. above, note 10, and below, ch. VIII-X.

VI

Intensive Involvement

The *Zohar's* vision of the overall study of *Pnimiyut haTorah* is not one of merely a formal acceptance in principle or of a transcendental acquaintance, but of an immanent and all-pervasive understanding and comprehension.

When R. Shneur Zalman of Liadi interprets the *Zohar's* precondition to the Messiainic redemption, as quoted above, to mean *limud be'iyun gadol davka* — an *intensive study* of, and *comprehensive deliberation* on *Pnimiyut haTorah*,[34] he follows clearly in the footsteps of the classic commentators preceding him:

"*'And because in the future Israel* lemit'am (*will*

---

34. Quoted by R. Dov Ber (*Mitteler Rebbe*) of Lubavitch, *Biurei Hazohar*, Introduction.

taste) *from the Tree of Life —*': Note the expression *lemit'am*. It implies that the meanings of the *Zohar's* teachings ultimately will become manifest in a mode of *tuv ta'am* (goodness of taste; good discernment; Psalms 119:66) to the point that every palate tasting it will desire it, as opposed to he who studies [the *Zohar*] superficially only. The latter will not sense its sweetness, while Scripture states '*Taste* and see that G-d is good' (Psalms 34:9).

"'*— they will leave the exile with* [*the Zohar*]': This is meant to be when they will taste (i.e., discern; comprehend) the meanings of its delightful teachings, as in these our own times which are the 'end of days' and the era of the redemption, as we wrote in section *Vayera* (*Zohar* I:folio) 117, see there."[35]

R. Sholom Buzaglo writes in his commentary on *Tikunei Zohar*:

"Note the expression '*when it will become manifest below*.' This clearly indicates that ... here below it will not be manifest until the 'last generation,' i.e., the 'end of days,' meaning quite specifically close to the era of the Messiah who will come on this account.[36]

"Verily, it is now hundreds of years already since the [*Zohar*] was revealed below, yet the descendant of

---

35. R. Shalom Buzaglo, *Hadrat Melech* on *Zohar* III:124b.
36. See also R. Shalom Buzaglo's introductions prefacing *Tikunei Zohar*.

David still has not come. But pay close attention to the text: it states *'yitparnessun* (they will be sustained; provided for) *by this work.'* The implication is that the profound teachings [of the *Zohar*] will be explicated — according to the premises revealed by R. Isaac Luria.[37]...

This is what is meant by [the term] *parnassah* (sustenance; provision), i.e., that they will understand and benefit from its light which is 'sweet to the soul and health to the bones' (Proverbs 16:24).

He who studies [the *Zohar* and *Pnimiyut haTorah*] superficially *(girsa be'alma)* will reap a good reward for his effort and sanctifies his soul in purity. The special remedy, however, by virtue of which 'you shall proclaim liberty,' is when *yitparnessun* (they will be sustained by) and study the meanings of the teachings [of the *Zohar*]."[38]

---

37. *Cf.* R. Chaim Vital, *Eitz Chayim* I:5; *Sha'ar Hahakdamot*, Hakdamah II; *Shomer Emunim* I:17.
38. *Kissei Melech* on the passage from *Tikunei Zohar* VI:23b quoted above.

VII

Modern Times

The progressive evolution in the manifestation and exposition of *Pnimiyut haTorah* reached a new milestone in our own age. For now, some two hundred years after the advent of the Baal Shem Tov and the Chassidic Movement, these teachings have been, and continue to be made available, not only in systematized form, in intelligible terminology and simplified exposition, but also translated into modern languages. This new development was initiated by R. Joseph Isaac Schneersohn of Lubavitch,[39] and intensified in every conceivable way by יבלח"א his successor, R. Menachem M. Schneerson of Lubavitch שליט"א.

This latest expansion has in effect removed the last

---

39. See *Likutei Sichot*, vol. III, pp. 374-6; *ibid.*, vol. XIII, p. 180;
    Sefer Hamaamarim-Bati Legani, vol. I, p. 307f.

barriers to the fullest and widest possible dissemination of
Pnimiyut haTorah — "the fountains of Chassidus which
were unlocked by R. Israel Baal Shem Tov, who envisaged
Chassidus as a stream of 'living waters,' growing deeper and
wider, until it should reach every segment of the Jewish
People and bring new inspiration and vitality into their daily
lives."[40]

In our own days, thus, the path has been cleared and
paved for the realization of R. Shimon bar Yochai's vision
that "when the days of the Messiah will be near at hand even
young children will happen to find the secrets of wisdom,"
— culminating in the era of "The earth shall be full of the
knowledge of G-d as the waters cover the sea" (Isaiah 11:9)
"And they shall teach no more every man his neighbour and
every man his brother saying 'Know G-d,' for they shall *all*
know Me, from the least of them unto the greatest of them"
(Jeremiah 31:33)![41]

40. Foreword by Lubavitcher Rebbe to the English translation of
    Tanya. See also *Likutei Sichot*, vol. XIII, p. 177*ff*.
41. See *Zohar* III:23a; Rambam, *Hilchot Melachim* 12:5

VIII

Achshur Darei?!

The fact that Jewish mysticism came into the open in ever-increasing stages only over the past 500 years, and especially in the last two centuries which followed the advent of the Baal Shem Tov and Chassidism, would seem to raise a problem.

The Talmud has an expression in the form of a rhetorical question: "*Achshur darei* — Is the present generation more fit?"[42] After all, the course of time is subject to a continuous deterioration in spiritual status: "If the earlier generations were like angels, we are but like plain humans; if they were like humans, we are like donkeys..."[43] How, then,

---

42. *Yevamot* 39b; *Chulin* 93b.
43. *Yerushalmi, Shekalim* 5:1; *Shabbat* 112b. Cf. *Eruvin* 53a; *Yoma* 9b; *Zohar* III:2a; and *Likutei Sichot*, vol. XV, p. 281, note 14.

is it possible that our later generations should merit a manifestation of *Pnimiyut haTorah* that was precluded from our much greater predecessors? How is it possible that in our lowly times we are told to study subjects that were kept from our ancestors who exceeded us in both their piety and their scholarship? What should make us more meritorious?

There are, however, two basic answers.[44]

The permission and obligation to study and promulgate *Pnimiyut haTorah* is an integral part of the evolutionary development of eras that culminates in the Messianic era, independent of the people and their status. Time does not stand still. Thus we are closer to the predetermined time of the Messianic redemption than our predecessors.[45] We live in the period called *ikvot Meshicha*, 'on the heels of Mashiach,'[46] the period of his imminent coming. The study of, and involvement with, *Pnimiyut haTorah*, is related to this, as already stated above (sect. II-IV), as follows:

a) As we move ever closer to the light of Mashiach, we already perceive a glimmer of that light. Ever more is revealed and manifested in anticipation of the final goal. The open manifestation of *Pnimiyut haTorah*, therefore, is an *effect* of the era itself.[47]

---

44. *Cf. Likutei Sichot*, vol. XV, p. 281*ff.*, and vol. XX, p. 172*ff.*

45. Scripture (Isaiah 60:22) states that the Messianic redemption will be "in its time," i.e., a prefixed time. That same verse, however, also states "I shall hasten it," which implies *before* the appointed time! The Talmud resolves the seeming contradiction: "If they are worthy, 'I shall hasten it;' if they are not worthy, it will be 'in its time.'" *Sanhedrin* 98a. *Cf. Zohar* I:116b*ff.*

46. For this term, and its significance, see *Sotah* 49b; *Or Hachayim* on Genesis 49:9, and *ibid.*, on Deuteronomy 7:12.

47. See *Likkutei Sichot* (English), vol. I:Bereishit, pp. 110-112.

b) *Pnimiyut haTorah* is not only an *effect* of *ikvot Meshicha*, but also a *preparation*, a cleansing and elevating process, to ready ourselves, to make us fit and receptive to the Messianic redemption with all the new revelations and manifestations that come with it.

We are indeed not greater or better than our predecessors. They superseded us in every respect. Nonetheless, they did not merit the Messianic redemption. *We* shall merit it, though not by virtue of being superior. We shall experience it either because the predetermined time of itself coincides with our own, or by virtue of the accumulative merit of all the generations up to our time. In the words of an ancient proverb,[48] we are "like a midget standing on the shoulders of a giant": though the midget is much smaller than the giant, by virtue of standing on his shoulders he can see much further.[49]

---

48. Cited in author's Foreword of *Shibalei Haleket*, see there.
49. See *Likkutei Sichot* (English), vol. III:Vayikra, p. 110.

IX

The Crown-Jewel

The very fact that we are inferior to our predecessors accounts for the change in the promulgation of *Pnimiyut haTorah*. *Pnimiyut haTorah* is the very core or essence of the Torah, its most sublime dimension. Thus one must indeed be most careful with it. There are very serious dangers in coping with its delicate and sensitive subjects. If one is unable to cope with these, he will come to harm. Hence all the words of caution, admonitions and restrictive measures by the sages of all times.[50]

At times, however, it becomes necessary to use precisely the most potent and normally dangerous methods. For example, radiation is very dangerous, and exposure to it may result in ill effects. Nonetheless, there are certain diseases

---

50. See above, notes 19-22, and also note 27.

where this selfsame exposure is their cure. And likewise with various other medications.[51]

R. Shneur Zalman of Liadi thus explains the well-known paradox of the *parah adumah* (red heifer) which "defiles those that are pure, and purifies those that are defiled"[52]: one and the same medication will cure the sick who need it, but harm the healthy who do not need it.[53] R. Menachem Mendel of Lubavitch (*Tzemach Tzedek*) applies this principle to our context: the earlier generations were strong and healthy in their *yirat Shamayim* (fear of G-d) and thus did not need the study of *Pnimiyut haTorah*, unlike our own generations when this study has become an obligatory necessity.[54] To understand this more clearly, there is a parable told by R. Shneur Zalman:[55]

Once upon a time there was a great and powerful king who had but one son. He sent his son to many places to be trained in all the arts and sciences. One day the king was informed that his son had fallen ill on some far-off island with a dangerous disease that perplexed his doctors. Immediately the king gathered the greatest medical experts to find a cure, but to no avail. Anxiety and frustration filled all in the kingdom, until one day a man appeared and said that he knew of an effective medicine. The alleged elixir, however, consisted of a unique and most precious stone grounded into

51. See *Likkutei Sichot* (English), vol. I:Bereishit, pp. 85-89.
52. See *Midrash Tehilim* 9:2. *Tanchuma*, Chukat:3, and in ed. Buber, par. 5.
53. *Maamarei Admur Hazaken* — 5563, vol. I:p. 237f.
54. *Or Hatorah*, Chukat, p. 777. See *Likutei Sichot*, vol. XX, p. 106f.
55. *Or Torah*, Hossafot, par. 91. See *The Great Maggid*, p. 117ff.; and cf. *Likutei Sichot*, vol. X, p. 237.

fine powder which had to be mixed with a liquid and then fed to the patient. After a thorough search, the king's servants could find but one stone of the type prescribed: the central and most precious jewel adorning the principal crown of the king.

The joy of finding this jewel was soon tempered by a great dilemma: the removal of the stone might cure the prince, but it would dim the very symbol of the royal majesty. To the king, however, nothing mattered as much as a cure for his only child. Thus he ordered that the jewel be removed and pounded into powder. In the meantime, however, the latest medical bulletins reported that the patient's condition had deteriorated to the point that he was unable to take in even liquids. His mouth could hardly be opened. The king's advisors thus thought it useless and senseless to destroy the stone and with it the crown's very glory. The king, however, insisted that they proceed, arguing that the slightest chance of getting a single drop of the elixir into the patient's mouth is worth the destruction of the crown-jewel.

The advisors protested: "For as long as your son was able to take in food and drink we agreed with you. Nothing is too precious to save his life. But now that his condition has worsened this much it is most doubtful, in fact unlikely, that he will be able to take in anything. Under these conditions it is surely not right to destroy the very diadem of the kingdom!"

The king replied: "If, Heaven forbid, my son should not live, what use do I have for the crown? Alternatively, if my son survives, surely that shall be my greatest glory: the life of an only son who exposed himself to dangers in order to obey his father's wish and excel in wisdom!"

Pnimiyut haTorah is the crown-jewel of the Torah, and the King's son, the people of Israel, in the lowly and diseased state of the present *galut*, is in dire need of that most precious life-giving elixir of *Pnimiyut haTorah* simplified and popularized to a level that all can understand it.

The truth of this analogy is seen and proven in the historical events and effects of the rise and spreading of Chassidut. Immediately prior to the Baal Shem Tov, European Jewry was very demoralized, verily in a state of physical, mental and spiritual stupor. There had been terrible pogroms and persecutions, intense sufferings on the physical level in addition to the demoralizing after-effects of the pseudo-Messianic adventures of those days. Then came R. Israel Baal Shem Tov and literally revived the people.[56]

There has hardly ever been a time of so many charismatic saints as the Baal Shem Tov and his disciples, the Maggid and his disciples, and their successors, who inspired their people in so comprehensive and penetrating a way that uplifted them spiritually and morally by means of the teachings and practices of Chassidism. And this life-giving elixir of *Pnimiyut haTorah* continues to this very day to inspire every kind of Jews throughout the world as nothing else. For the "soul of the Torah" speaks directly to, and affects, the "soul of every Jew."[57]

Thus it is precisely the status of spiritual degradation,

---

56. Note the comment of R. Pinchas of Koretz that R. Israel Baal Shem Tov reawakened and revived the souls of Israel in general, and of every Jew in particular; *ms.* quoted in *Migdal Oz*, p. 358*f.* See *Likutei Sichot*, vol. II, p. 516; and *The Great Maggid*, p. 29.

57. See *Likutei Sichot*, vol. V, p. 302.

the very darkness of the present *galut*, that requires the medicine of the most sublime aspects of the Torah to cure it.[58]

---

58. Note the words of the Vilna Gaon that specifically the preoccupation with *Pnimiyut haTorah* offers protection against the *yetzer hara; Even Shelemah* VIII:27. See also his comment on Isaiah 6:10, in *Kol Eliyahu*, p. 60*f.*

X

Tradition and Change

To be sure, this argument, which depends on the introduction of an innovation, was criticized already in the
days of the Baal Shem Tov: "Our ancestors and predecessors
did not study *Pnimiyut haTorah*, and therefore we do not
need it either. If the *status quo ante* of getting along without
it was good enough for *them*, it is also good enough for *us*".
This critique, however, is inherently inconsistent and
fallacious.

The inconsistency is readily seen in our very own
human reality. "A lover of *kessef* (silver; money) is never
satisfied with *kessef*" (Ecclesiastes 5:9). Thus it is human
nature that "He who has a hundred, wants to turn them into
two hundred; and if has two hundred, he wants to turn them
into four hundred."[59] On the physical level none of us turns

---

59. *Kohelet Rabba* 1:13; and *ibid.*, 3:10.

to the past to satisfy himself with the lifestyle of our predecessors. In the physical realm we do not say "if it was good
enough for our ancestors it is good enough for us," but we
seek out the latest inventions and discoveries in medicine and
technology.

The same must then apply to the spiritual realm as
well. Indeed, our sages state that the word *kessef* is also used
to designate *mitzvot*; thus they interpret the above-cited
verse of Ecclesiastes to mean that he who truly loves Torah
and *mitzvot* will never be satisfied with what he has: he will
continually seek to add to these and to enhance them ever
more.[60] As new challenges confront us every day, we cannot
suffice with the religious lifestyle of yesteryear.

R. Ya'akov Yosef of Polnoy thus comments on the
Mishnah,[61] "Be a tail to lions rather than a head to foxes":
the difference between a lion and a fox is that the former
looks ahead while the latter keeps turning backward![62] And
in this vein he expounds the Scriptural verse that the prophet
Elijah, the precursor of Mashiach, "will turn the heart of the
fathers *to the children*" (Malachi 3:24), quoting a trenchant
comment by R. Nachman of Kossov: "Do not turn to the
ovot" (the mediums in necromancy; Leviticus 19:31) can
also be read, by changing but one vowel, "Do not turn to the
avot (ancestors);"[63] that is, when people criticize your addi-

---

60. *Kohelet Rabba* on Ecclesiastes 5:9. *Makot* 10b.
61. *Avot* 4:15.
62. See *Shir Rabba* 2:15.
63. This interpretation *bederech mussar* is to be found already
    earlier, in the Foreword of R. Israel Yaffe, *Or Yisrael*, attributed
    to R. Mosheh ben David of Vilna. *Cf.* also Ecclesiastes 7:10, as
    interpreted by R. Chaim of Tchernovitz, *Sha'ar Hatefilah*, s.v.
    She'eilah Uteshuvah (a responsum to refute a critique in *Noda*

tional, and seemingly excessive, acts of piety, saying that these were not practiced by your ancestors, the retort is simply — *al tifnu el ha'avot*! R. Nachman still added the rhetorical question: "In practical terms, did your parents and grandparents succeed in bringing Mashiach?!"

R. Ya'akov Yosef concludes that this is the meaning of the verse in Malachi: in the days of the prophet Elijah, the parents will acknowledge that their ways were insufficient. Thus they will adopt the ways of their children who chose better by accepting upon themselves additional acts of piety and restrictions that go beyond the requirements of the law.[64]

The adoption of additional acts of piety and supplementary restrictions does not stand in violation of the principles of "Do not forsake the instruction of your mother" (Proverbs 1:8) and "Give heed to the customs of your ancestors that have come down to you."[65] On the contrary, it is part of the Biblical precept "Guard My charge" (Leviticus 18:30) which means the obligation to take precautionary measures for the preservation and guarding of the Divine instructions of the Torah.[66] If this applies in all times, how

---

Biyehudah against alleged innovations by the mystics; in recent edition, Jerusalem 1989, p. 395).

64. *Toldot Ya'akov Yosef*, Bo, on Exodus 13:12-14 (ed. Jerusalem 1960, pp. 160 and 163).

65. See R. Mosheh of Tirani, *Bet Elokim*, Sha'ar Hayesodot, ch. 38; and *Sdei Chemed*, Kuntres Hakelalim, *s.v.* minhag:klal 38 (ed. Kehot, vol. II, p. 905). See *Even Shelemah* 11:7; and *cf. Shulchan Aruch*, Yoreh De'ah, sect. 214.

66. *Yevamot* 21a. See *Likkutei Sichot* (English), vol. III:Vayikra, p. 124*ff.*; and *ibid.*, p. 139*ff.*

much more so nowadays when there is a spiritual deterioration of the generations.[67]

This, indeed, is the classical definition that our sages give for the terms *chassid* and *chassidut*,[68] and that is what Chassidism seeks to instill in all Jews: a sense of holiness, a sense of piety, that takes us beyond minimal requirements and customary norms; a taste and consciousness of G-dliness that whets the appetite for ever more and will not be satisfied until the experience of the ultimate manifestation of the Messianic age when the whole earth shall be filled with the knowledge of G-d as the waters cover the sea,[69] for "the glory of G-d shall be revealed (to the point) that all *flesh* shall see.." (Isaiah 40:5) — in a truly empirical way.[70]

---

67. See the comment of the Vilna Gaon quoted in *Even Shelemah* XI:7, explicitly applying this principle to the present deteriorating conditions of the *galut*. Precisely these conditions make it imperative to study *Pnimiyut haTorah*, the esoteric dimension of the Torah. *Cf.* R. Simchah Bunim of Pshizcha, *Torat Simchah*, p. 57.

68. See *Encyclopaedia Talmudit*, *s.v.* Chassid. See also *Tikunei Zohar*, Intr.:1b; *Zohar* II:214b; and *ibid.*, III:222b. *Cf. Likutei Sichot*, vol. XI, pp. 85 and 87; *Kuntres Inyanah shel Torat Hachassidut*, ch. 1.

69. See above, note 41.

70. See *Likutei Sichot*, vol. XV, p. 44.

BIBLIOGRAPHY
and
INDEXES

BIBLIOGRAPHY

AVODAT HAKODESH, R. Chaim Yosef David Azulay (*Chida*), Brooklyn NY 1945

BEN PORAT YOSSEF, R. Yaakov Yosef of Polnoy, New York 1954

BET ELOKIM, R. Mosheh of Tirani (*Mabit*), Warsaw 1831

BI'UREI HAZOHAR, R. Dov Ber of Lubavitch, Brooklyn NY 1955

CHIDUSHEI HARITVA, R. Yomtov ben Abraham Ashbeli, New York 1966

CHOVOT HALEVOVOT, R. Bachya ibn Pakuda, Diessen 1946

DEGEL MACHANEH EPHRAYIM, R. Mosheh Chaim Ephrayim of Sudylkov, Jerusalem 1963

DERASHOT HARAN, R. Nissim Gerondi, Jerusalem 1973

DEVASH LEFI, R. Chaim Yosef David Azulay (*Chida*), Jerusalem 1962

EITZ CHAYIM, R. Chaim Vital, ed. Warsaw, Tel Aviv 1975

EVEN SHELEMAH, Anthology of teachings of R. Elijah, the Vilna Gaon, compiled by R. Shmuel of Slutzk, Jerusalem 1960

GEVUROT HASHEM, R. Judah Loew (*Maharal*), New York 1969

HAYOM YOM, R. Menachem M. Schneerson of Lubavitch, Brooklyn NY 1961

IGERET HAKODESH, part IV of TANYA (*s.v.*)

IGERET HATESHUVAH, part III of TANYA (*s.v.*)

IGERET TEYMAN, IGROT HARAMBAM ed. Y. Kapach, Jerusalem 1972

IKKARIM, R. Joseph Albo, Vilna n.d.

KAD HAKEMACH, R. Bachya ben Asher, New York 1960

KETER SHEM TOV, Anthology of teachings of R. Israel Baal Shem Tov, compiled by R. Aaron of Apt, ed. Kehot, Brooklyn NY 1987

KOL ELIYAHU, R. Elijah, the Vilna Gaon, Brooklyn NY n.d.

KUNTRES EITZ HACHAYIM, R. Sholom Dov Ber of Lubavitch, Brooklyn NY 1956

KUNTRES INYANAH SHEL TORAT HACHASSIDUT, R. Menachem M. Schneerson of Lubavitch, Brooklyn NY 1971

KUZARY, R. Judah Halevi, Tel Aviv 1959

LIKUTEI AMARIM, see MAGGID DEVARAV LEYA'AKOV

LIKUTEI DIBURIM, R. Yosef Yitzchak of Lubavitch, Brooklyn NY 1957

LIKUTEI LEVI YITZCHAK-ZOHAR, R. Levi Yitzchak Schneerson, Brooklyn NY 1970-71

LIKUTEI SICHOT, R. Menachem M. Schneerson of Lubavitch, Brooklyn NY 1962-89

LIKUTEI TORAH, R. Shneur Zalman of Liadi, Brooklyn NY 1965

LIKUTIM YEKARIM, Anthology of teachings of Baal Shem Tov, Maggid, and others, ed. Toldot Aharon, Jerusalem 1974

LIMUD HACHASSIDUT, R. Yosef Yitzchak of Lubavitch, Brooklyn NY 1956

MAAMAREI ADMUR HAZAKEN-5563, R. Shneur Zalman of Liadi, Brooklyn NY 1981-2

MAGGID DEVARAV LEYA'AKOV, Anthology of teachings of R. Dov Ber (*Maggid*) of Mezhirech, ed. Kehot, Brooklyn NY 1979

MAYIM RABIM-5636, R. Shmuel of Lubavitch, Brooklyn NY 1946

MEGILAT HAMEGALEH, R. Abraham bar Chiya, Berlin 1924

MENORAT HAMAOR, R. Israel ibn Al-Nakawa, New York 1929-32

MEVO SHE'ARIM, R. Chaim Vital, Tel Aviv 1961

MIDBAR KEDEMOT, R. Chaim Yosef David Azulay (*Chida*), Jerusalem 1962

MOREH NEVUCHIM, R. Mosheh Maimonides, Jerusalem 1960

NETIVOT OLAM, R. Judah Loew (*Maharal*), London 1961

NETZACH YISRAEL, R. Judah Loew (*Maharal*), New York 1969

OR HACHAMAH, R. Abraham Azulay, Przemysl 1896

OR HAME'IR, R. Ze'ev Wolf of Zhitomir, Lemberg 1850

OR HATORAH, R. Menachem Mendel (*Tzemach Tzedek*) of Lubavitch, Brooklyn NY 1960 *e.s.*

OR NE'ERAV, R. Mosheh Cordovero, Fuerth 1701

OR TORAH, Anthology of teachings of R. Dov Ber, Maggid of Mezhirech, ed. Kehot, Brooklyn NY 1979

PARDES RIMONIM, R. Mosheh Cordovero, Jerusalem 1962

PELACH HARIMON, R. Menachem Azaryah de Fano, Jerusalem 1962

RAMBAN AL HATORAH, R. Mosheh Nachmanides, Jerusalem 1959

R. BACHAYA AL HATORAH, R. Bachya ben Asher, Jerusalem 1959

REISHIT CHOCHMAH, R. Eliyahu de Vidas, Amsterdam 1708

SEFER BAAL SHEM TOV, Anthology of teachings of R. Israel Baal Shem Tov, compiled by R. Shimon Menachem Mendel of Gavartchov, Landsberg 1948

SEFER CHAREIDIM, R. Eleazar Azkari, Jerusalem 1958

SEFER CHASSIDIM, R. Yehudah Hachassid, ed. Margolius, Jerusalem 1957

SEFER HACHINUCH, R. Aharon Halevi of Barcelona, New York 1962

SEFER HACHIZYONOT, R. Chaim Vital, Jerusalem 1954
SEFER HAGILGULIM, R. Chaim Vital, Vilna 1886
SEFER HALIKUTIM AL TNACH, R. Meir Papirash and R. Shalom Sharabi,
   Jerusalem 1981
SEFER HAMITZVOT, R. Mosheh Maimonides, Jerusalem 1959
SEFER HASICHOT 5700, R. Yosef Yitzchak of Lubavitch, Brooklyn NY
   1956
SHA'AR HAGILGULIM, R. Chaim Vital, Tel Aviv 1963
SHA'AR HAHAKDAMOT, R. Chaim Vital, Tel Aviv 1961
SHA'AR HAKOLEL, R. Abraham David Lavut, (Israel) 1968
SHA'AR HAMITZVOT, R. Chaim Vital, Tel Aviv 1962
SHA'AR HATEFILAH, R. Chaim of Tchernowitz, Warsaw 1874
SHA'AR RUACH HAKODESH, R. Chaim Vital, Tel Aviv 1963
SHA'AREI KEDUSHAH, R. Chaim Vital, Horodna 1994
SHEMONAH PERAKIM, R. Mosheh Maimonides, Jerusalem 1968
SHIBALEI HALEKET, R. Tzidkiyah dei Mansi, New York 1959
SHI'UR KOMAH, R. Mosheh Cordovero, Jerusalem 1966
SH'NEI LUCHOT HABERIT, R. Isaiah Horowitz, Jerusalem 1963
SHOMER EMUNIM, R. Joseph Ergas, Jerusalem 1965
SHULCHAN ARUCH ARIZAL, Jerusalem 1961
SHULCHAN ARUCH HARAV, R. Shneur Zalman of Liadi, Brooklyn NY
   1960-8
SIDUR IM DACH, R. Shneur Zalman of Liadi, Brooklyn NY 1965
SIMCHAT YISRAEL, Anthology of teachings of R. Simchah Bunem of
   Pshyzcha, ed. R. Israel Berger, Pietrokov 1910
TANYA, R. Shneur Zalman of Liadi, Brooklyn NY 1965
TAV CHAYIM, R. Chaim Korin, Brooklyn NY 1959
TESHUVOT HARASHBA, R. Shelomoh ben Abraham Adret, Bnei Berak
   1958
TESHUVOT MIN HASHAMAYIM, R. Jacob of Marvege, Jerusalem 1957
TIFERET YISRAEL, R. Judah Loew (Maharal), New YUork 1969
TOLA'AT YA'AKOV, R. Meir ibn Gabbai, Warsaw 1876
TOLDOT YA'AKOV YOSEF, R. Ya'akov Yosef of Polnoy, Jerusalem 1960
TORAH OR, R. Shneur Zalman of Liadi, Brooklyn NY 1954
TORAT HACHASSIDUT, R. Yosef Yitzchak of Lubavitch, Brooklyn NY
   1945
TORAT SHMUEL-V:5638, R. Shmuel of Lubavitch, Brooklyn NY 1945
TORAT SIMCHAH, see SIMCHAT YISRAEL
TZAFNAT PANE'ACH, R. Ya'akov Yosef of Polnoy, New York 1954
TZAVA'AT HARIVASH, Anthology of teachings of Baal Shem Tov, ed.
   Kehot, Brooklyn NY 1982

Index of Biblical and Rabbinic Quotations

TALMUD

Maimonides

Shulchan Aruch

Index of Subjects